ANCHOR POINT

ANCHOR POINT

How to
Lead with Faith
Find Strength and
Rebuild with Hope
AFTER CRISIS

A Disaster Recovery Guide for Pastors and Ministry Leaders

JOHN W. CROWDER

invite PRESS

Plano, Texas

ISBN Paperback 9781963265620, eBook 9781963265637

All scripture quotations unless noted otherwise are from The Holy Bible, English Standard Version® (ESV), copyright © 2001 by Crossway Bibles, a publishing ministry of Good News Publishers. Used by permission. All rights reserved.

Scripture quotations marked KJV are from the King James or Authorized Version of the Bible, which is in public domain.

Scripture quotations marked NASB are from the New American Standard Bible®, Copyright © 1960, 1962, 1963, 1968, 1971, 1972, 1973, 1975, 1977, 1995, 2020 by The Lockman Foundation. All rights reserved. Used by permission. (www.Lockman.org)

Scripture quotations marked NIV are taken from THE HOLY BIBLE, NEW INTERNATIONAL VERSION®, NIV® Copyright © 1973, 1978, 1984, 2011 by Biblica, Inc.™ Used by permission of Zondervan. All rights reserved worldwide.

25 26 27 28 29 30 31 32 33 34—10 9 8 7 6 5 4 3 2 1

MANUFACTURED in the UNITED STATES of AMERICA

CONTENTS

FOREWORD

Disasters strike fast—but recovery is slow. Recovery unfolds in the debris-strewn streets or gutted homes and also in the hearts, relationships, and spiritual resilience of every individual and community impacted. This book, *Anchor Point*, offers an extraordinary and honest look at the immediate, short-term, and long-term impacts a disaster leaves in its wake—and why understanding each phase matters deeply.

Anchor Point is more than a title. It's a motif. It reminds us that in times of chaos, people are looking for something steady, something grounded, something anchored. In these pages, Crowder gives us just that: steady guidance rooted in lived experience and practical truth. He helps you know, so you can lead.

Leadership in disaster recovery is not simply about showing up with the right gear or signing up for the first available assignment. It's about showing up with the right expectations. In *An-*

chor Point, Crowder sets realistic expectations for every phase of recovery—so pay attention. Whether you are a pastor, nonprofit leader, or community volunteer, this book is for you.

You will find practical advice and steps coupled with emotional direction—for the leader trying to do the right thing, for the community learning how to breathe again, and for the outside volunteers stepping into stories they do not yet understand. This is not just a manual—it is a map for the heart and mind alike.

One of the greatest strengths of *Anchor Point* is how it lifts up concepts often overlooked. Crowder dispenses wisdom on important aspects of life and leadership which are seldom taught—like the "ministry of presence"—the art of simply being there when words fail. Or how to build a community that doesn't just survive but helps others recover, too. He reminds us that leadership after disaster isn't about having all the answers, but about being an answer—present, compassionate, and rooted.

Key themes emerge throughout the book: the importance of setting expectations early; the need to plug into something bigger than yourself; the value of knowing your community and its emergency leaders before the disaster strikes; and the transformational power of building relationships that carry people through the months and years to come.

Crowder also touches a sacred space: recovery work is spiritual work. It's not just chainsaws and cleanup—it's coffee shared with the grieving. It's laughter in the middle of mud. It's faith rising up from the ashes of loss. That is the ministry of presence. That is what *Anchor Point* calls us to.

In my work, I've seen firsthand how this kind of leadership transforms towns and people. And I've seen the cost of rushing in without wisdom. This book is a gift because it helps people walk wisely—and walk together.

So whether you're preparing your church to respond, organizing a local disaster response team, or simply trying to make sense of what recovery actually looks like, you've found a vital companion. *Anchor Point* will serve not only as a guide but as grounding—bringing clarity when confusion reigns and purpose when all seems lost.

Let these pages challenge you. Let them equip you. Most of all, let them remind you that the road to recovery is not just possible—it is attainable by people willing to lead with courage, compassion, and conviction.

Rand Jenkins
President / CEO
On Mission Network
OnMissionNetwork.org

AUTHOR'S NOTE

"You have multiplied, O Lord my God, your wondrous deeds and your thoughts toward us; none can compare with you! I will proclaim and tell of them, yet they are more than can be told." Psalm 40:5

It is not possible to number the stories that should be told about people affected by the West Fertilizer Plant explosion on April 17, 2013 and the subsequent disaster recovery efforts. Hundreds of people could tell thousands of stories that are worthy of remembering and recording. I cannot take on that monumental task, nor would I presume to attempt it. Instead, I will tell my own story, for it is the one I know best. I do not intend to leave anyone out or minimize anyone's contribution. Nor is it my intent to compare my suffering to that of anyone else. I am eager, however, to share my story for three reasons. First, I have been overwhelmed and amazed by the goodness of God, and like King David, I want to "tell of all his wonderous works (Psalm 105:2b)." Second, I want to chronicle what I experienced in the hope that it will enable others to have a greater understanding of the events that took place. Finally, I want to use my story as a backdrop to highlight some of the lessons that could help other leaders walk through disasters with their communities. It is the third reason that serves as the primary motivation for this book. I hope to pass along lessons learned from personal experience that will help others navigate the frightening, disorienting experience of disaster recovery.

After more than a decade of walking alongside other leaders as their communities struggled through disaster recovery, the observation that troubles me the most is how the proverbial wheel gets reinvented each time a disaster occurs. In each case, local leaders, particularly ministers, must learn how to coordinate relief efforts, communicate with officials, organize volunteers, assess needs, deal with personal loss while leading with hope, etc. Until the world seemingly falls apart around us, we have no reason to study such things. Then, when we are most vulnerable and under unthinkable stress, we must scramble to learn what we can and find ways to get our communities through the chaos. Precious time is lost, and a tremendous toll is taken on the physical, emotional, and spiritual well-being of the leader. This explains why so many ministers leave their posts soon after their disaster recovery experience. It is my prayer that this book might help pastors and ministry leaders be prepared or at least have an accessible resource that will help them spend less time on reinventing the wheel and be able to put more of their energy into leading and caring for their people.

INTRODUCTION

The storm raged for at least two weeks. Through pain and exhaustion, the sailors on the little ship fought the forces of nature. Although they feared for their lives, they continued the struggle to keep their vessel afloat. They were helplessly tossed back and forth in a darkness that lasted for days. They had no food and had lost most of their provisions. Eventually, all hope was lost. All they could do was drop their anchors and pray for a new day to dawn. The one thing they did have was a leader. There was in their midst a person whom God could use to encourage them, bring peace, and restore hope. As Luke records the story in Acts 27, Paul stepped up in the chaos and helped the people hang on until things calmed down again. How was he able to accomplish that timely and essential ministry? He had his own anchors. Just as the crew dropped four anchors to steady the ship (Acts 27:29), Paul was personally anchored by four truths. Those anchor points allowed him to lead with faith and courage. We can see Paul's anchor points in his encouraging speech to the sailors in Acts 27:22–25.

> *Yet now I urge you to take heart, for there will be no loss of life among you, but only of the ship. For this very night there stood before me an angel of the God to whom I belong and whom I worship, and he said, "Do not be afraid, Paul; you must stand before Caesar. And behold, God has granted you all those who sail with you." So take heart, men, for I have faith in God that it will be exactly as I have been told.*

- Paul was *courageous* because he trusted in the **presence of God**. He had been visited by an angel. The angel represented God's presence on that ship.

- Paul had *vision* because he knew the **purpose of God** for his life. Paul knew they would survive the shipwreck because he had a purpose to fulfill in Rome.

- Paul had *peace* because he could rest in the **protection of God**. The angel reassured him that God would protect him and the whole crew.

- Paul had *hope* because he relied on the **promises of God**. Based on the promises he received from the angel, Paul inspired the sailors by telling them to "take heart" because he knew God would keep His promises.

Paul was able to lead others through crises because his life was steadied by those anchor points. An anchor point is a secure place on which you can rely. It provides a point of reference that is essential in stressful or frightening times. In archery, an anchor point is a spot on the archer's chin against which the drawing hand is placed to stabilize the archer's aim. The archer can shoot with consistency by returning to that anchor point with every shot. In repelling or fall arrest systems, the anchor point is a secure location where gear can be attached to prevent falls. In firefighting, an anchor point is a barrier that cannot burn and is used as a defensible starting place for constructing a fire line. Without an anchor point, firefighters risk getting trapped by the fire if it spreads around them. There are also anchor points in audio mixing, video editing, and graphic design. In those cases, the term signifies a reference point that is the beginning place for making adjustments.

Paul's anchor points were all based on provisions of God. Because he trusted the Lord, Paul knew he could rely on God's presence, purpose, protection, and promises. The same anchor points are available to you today. Even if you are called on to lead through terrible storms you can do so with courage, vision, peace, and hope just like Paul.

CHAPTER 1
THE DARKEST NIGHT

"No words adequately describe the courage that was displayed on that deadly night." President Barack Obama [1]

The Day Our World Changed

When I got up and started my day on Wednesday, April 17, 2013, I knew it would be a day that would mark a major change in my family and how we lived our lives. Ashley is our only child. Ever since she was five years old, she has played one sport or another. My wife Lisa and I were in the stands for almost every event. She started with T-ball and grew into softball. She also played basketball and volleyball, and she ran track. This was her senior year at West High School. It was the end of track season, and she had qualified for the area track meet in Bryan, TX. I got up that morning feeling a little old and very sentimental as I realized that when she crossed the finished line at the end of the

---

1. President Barack Obama, speaking at the national memorial service held in Waco, TX on April 25, 2013, in honor of the fallen firefighters from West.

mile relay that night, she might be finished with all her sporting events, and our family dynamics would change forever. We would have no more opportunities to cheer her on when she was winning or to be there for her when the game did not go her way. We would have no more road trips to track meets or away games. Never again would I have that amazing feeling of pride that used to make me want to stand up and tell everyone in the stadium, "That's my kid!" Athletics had always been a big part of our family, and now that was all going away. It felt like just yesterday we took our little girl to that first T-ball "try-out." Now she was about to run what might be her final race, and soon after that, she would graduate and leave home. It was hard for me to picture what life would be like without sports, and I could not bring myself to even contemplate life without my baby girl at home. I moved slowly that morning, dreading the changes that were coming. I was eager to see her run, but I wanted that final event to last as long as possible, just in case that finish line marked the end of her childhood.

Ashley did run that last race, and she did well. The finality of the event was not lost on her. She and her teammates ended the evening and their high school sports activities with tears and hugs. After a few words of encouragement and assuring Ashley that we were proud of her, we got in the car, and she got on the school bus. We ate dinner in Bryan and started the familiar journey of a little less than a hundred miles to our home in West, Texas. That was a journey we never completed. We never got to go to our home again.

I was recovering from a recent injury, so I did not drive that night. Lisa was driving while I did what you do in a car when you are not driving: I was on my cell phone looking at Facebook. A few minutes after 7:30 p.m. I noticed a post that said the West fertilizer plant was on fire. "Oh, what a shame," I thought. "That's too bad. I hope the fire department can put it out quickly." I was naïve and failed to recognize the gravity of the situation. I was not at all aware of how dangerous a fire at a fertilizer plant could be. I thought there was just another structure fire, and I knew we had some highly qualified firefighters who would take care of it and protect us like they always do. A few minutes later the phone rang.

The life changes that we experienced at the track meet a couple of hours earlier paled in comparison to the news I received on that phone call. Dr. Larry Sparks, who is one my deacons, told me the fertilizer plant had exploded. He told me many houses were destroyed, and there would be many people who were hurt. When tragedy strikes, our minds often utilize certain defense mechanisms to lessen the blow. Shock is a scary experience. My mind went hazy, and I could not fully comprehend what I was hearing. I knew that Larry was telling me that something awful had happened, but it did not sink in that he was also warning us that we could not return home. I told Lisa what Larry had said, and she immediately thought of our helpless little lap dog at home. Princess was a little white puff ball, who was spoiled rotten and in constant need of attention. She was part of the family. And we knew that she was all alone after the most frightening experience we could imagine. We knew that we had to get home to take care of her. We knew she had to be scared, and we prayed that she had not run off or been badly injured or worse. I told Larry we would get to West as quickly as we could so we could check on Princess and then see what we could do to help.

The next few minutes are not clear in my memory as that mental haze settled in, protecting me from the horrors of our reality. I do remember that Larry was concerned enough to call back. Trying to help me understand how bad things were, he told me in no uncertain terms that we probably did not have a house to go to, and it was too late to worry about the dog. He also informed me that the authorities were already evacuating our side of town because a second explosion was likely imminent. As the news forced its way through my confusion and finally became clear to me, I was overcome with grief and anxiety.

As soon as I could formulate the words, I turned to Lisa and I told her, "There is no way to know what we will find when we get home. It's going to be bad. No matter what, just remember that Ashley is ok, and we all have each other. That's what matters most." About that time, Ashley texted me saying the students on the bus had heard about the explosion, so I called her immediately. I stressed to her the same thing I had just told Lisa. We still had each other and that was most important. She agreed but immediately expressed her concern for Princess. I guess we were all worried about that dog, but I could not offer any assurance that she would be alright. We had no way of knowing what happened to her or our house.

As scared as I was about losing our home and maybe everything we owned, I also knew that we were fortunate. With an explosion as bad as the one we were hearing about, there would certainly be casualties and fatalities. I knew that other families were suffering and had lost much more than we had. Even if we lost everything we owned, we had each other. My heart broke for those who would not be able to say that about their own loved ones.

We were still about forty-five minutes away from home. I texted our extended family and the guys in my covenant group. I told them what little I knew and asked them to begin praying.

I remember receiving a phone call from Dr. Paul Stripling, who was a great friend and mentor. I remember talking with our associate pastor, Phil Immicke, a few times. I also remember asking my brother to make sure that my mother knew we were alright, and he assured me she already knew. Other than that, I honestly cannot remember all the calls and texts that I handled as I juggled my phone and Lisa's phone and did the best I could to keep up with all that was happening.

Like most Wednesday nights, we had a church full of people that evening. When the explosion happened, my chairman of deacons, Dan Moss, was leading the adult Bible study; Phil Immicke was meeting with the teenagers; and our children's workers were leading activities for the kids. At the moment of the blast, some of our elementary-aged boys were outside playing kickball, and the shockwave knocked them to the ground even though the church is almost a mile from the plant. Dan dismissed the adults, and Phil gathered all the students and children in the sanctuary. He immediately began to coordinate our emergency response. He made sure no one was seriously injured and helped parents find their kids or make other arrangements for them. One of the calls I got from him on our way back to town was about whether we should keep the children at the church or take them somewhere else. I told him they should stay where they were so parents would know how to find their kids. Soon after I gave him that advice, he was instructed by the authorities that our part of town was being evacuated, and he had to get everyone out of the church. Phil has a military background and law enforcement training, so we were glad that he was the one in charge. He was able to use his training and experience to help our people deal with an event that was more terrifying and tragic than any of us ever expected to face. I hated the fact that I was not at the church to help handle things, but I knew the church was in good hands.

It was good that Lisa was driving that night. I could not have handled the communication that I needed to take care of had I been driving. Besides that, concentrating on the road kept Lisa's mind off what we might find once we got home.

When we finally reached Waco, where Highway 6 meets Interstate 35, I got another clue about how serious things really were. I-35, which runs right up the middle of Texas, is one of the busiest highways in the country. I have lived close to I-35 my whole life, but that was the first time I had ever seen it with almost no cars on it. I do not know whether officials were encouraging people to stay off the highway or if everyone was at home glued to their televisions, but there were no personal vehicles on the road from Waco to West. Instead, the highway was full of first responders on their way to help. Every vehicle we saw was an emergency vehicle of one kind or another. Lights flashed all around us as law enforcement, EMS (Emergency Medical Services), rescue, ambulance, and fire vehicles of all shapes and sizes made their way to West. They had come from all over the state and were rushing to help the people who were my friends and neighbors. Hundreds of heroes were converging on my little town to take care of the people I had been called to serve and grown to love. We turned on our hazard lights and joined in the high-speed processional.

When we got to the southern edge of town, there were so many emergency vehicles moving around that we knew we could not get into town. The bus that Ashley was on could not get in either. West High School was just a couple of blocks from the fertilizer plant, and the school was badly damaged. Even if they could have maneuvered through all the chaos to make their way to the school, the track coaches knew the school would not be a safe place to take the students. Athletic Director David Woodard and the other coaches kept the safety of our students as their top priority and did a great job taking care of them. The athletes and coaches used cell phones to stay in touch with parents as the bus took students to their parents at various meeting places that were far enough away from town that we knew they would be safe. Lisa and I arranged to meet the bus a few miles out of town at the Kolars' house. The bus got held up for a while looking for parents elsewhere and all we could do was stand outside the house and wait, worry, and pray. It seemed like an eternity while we anxiously anticipated being reunited with Ashley.

During that time, my brother Richard was somehow able to get into the north part of town where our house was, and he took some pictures of the house and texted them to me. I can still see those images in my mind when I think about that night. The garage door was blown in and laid on the ground, folded in half. There was a crack across our front wall and part of that wall looked as if it could fall at any moment. And then I saw the picture that almost made my knees buckle: my front door and the panels that surrounded it had been blown into my living room. The door that had always stood in defense of my home and protected my family was now resting on top of my overturned recliner. Had I been at home that evening, I'm sure that chair is where I would have been. There is no way to know if I could have survived that heavy door landing on top of me. The other pictures my brother sent showed the interior of the house where the windows had shattered, all the ceilings had fallen in, and insulation covered everything in the house.

7

Finally, the bus brought Ashley to us. She jumped off the bus and ran to us at full speed with her arms outstretched. We ran to meet her and hugged her tightly as she and her mother burst into tears. There may have a tear or two lingering at the corners of my eyes as well. It was so good to be back together.

As we celebrated our reunion, we learned that Princess had been found and was ok. Hunter Johnson is a young man who grew up in our church, and our families have been friends for many years. He lived a few miles north of town. When he heard the explosion, he quickly came to West and went from house to house in our neighborhood making sure everyone was alright. When he got to our house, Princess was wandering around outside and came up to him. He picked her up and then made sure that we were not inside. Once he knew we were not home, he checked on some other homes nearby and sent word to Ashley that he had Princess.

We quickly arranged for Lisa and Ashley to go to Rusty and Michelle Johnson's house. The Johnsons are incredibly generous people who have great compassion. Rusty is one of my deacons and one of my closest friends. It was perfectly within his character to invite us to stay at his home for as long as necessary. Once I knew that Lisa and Ashley were safe and would be well cared for, I told Lisa I had to go into town to see what I could do to help. She was worried about me and hesitated for a moment, but I explained that there really was no choice. I had to do whatever I could to help. I am blessed with an incredibly understanding and supportive wife, so she told me goodbye and asked me to be careful. I left and went as quickly as possible to the community center, which was being used as an emergency command center. I worked until the early morning hours alongside my friends and neighbors. As we worked, we learned more about the explosion, but it would be many weeks until we learned all that actually happened on that darkest of nights.

The Darkest Night

The first call about the fire at the West Fertilizer Company went out at 7:29 p.m. Members of the volunteer fire department responded immediately. As the firefighters arrived, leaders in the department made plans and coordinated their efforts. More help was requested, and a strategy was quickly formed and implemented. These valiant volunteers had spent all day at work and were finally able to relax a little bit when they had to drop everything and stand in the gap between danger and their community. Taking their positions with courage, they protected their families and friends.

Our EMS building was just a few blocks from the plant. That night a class was being conducted there in which first responders were being trained to be paramedics. Some of the people in that class were firefighters from other towns who had come into West for the specialized training. When the fire broke out, they immediately jumped into action. Some of them went to the plant and began working alongside our local firefighters, and some of the others went across the street to the nursing home. They joined forces with the nursing home staff and our local EMS crew to evacuate the residents. As a result of their actions, many lives were saved.

The firefighters who responded that night put their own lives on the line to ensure that others might have a future. Later that year, the Dallas Morning News named the West first responders

"Texans of the Year." By all accounts, that designation was well-deserved. We will always be grateful to our first responders who protected us. Gov. Greg Abbott said of them, "Some people are alive today because of those heroes. West, as a town, is better and it will live forever because of those heroes."[2]

At 7:51 p.m., 22 minutes after the initial fire call, the building that was on fire collapsed. It was a wooden structure in which ammonium nitrate was stored. When the fire caused the building to collapse, heavy debris detonated the ammonium nitrate. In 1995, only 3.5 tons of ammonium nitrate were used to blow up the Alfred P. Murrah Federal Building in Oklahoma City. The explosion that occurred in West involved 28–34 tons of ammonium nitrate. That explosion was the equivalent of almost 20,000 pounds of dynamite. It was so powerful that the U.S. Geological Survey near Lake Whitney registered it as a 2.1-magnitude earthquake. It left a crater just under one hundred feet wide and ten feet deep, completely obliterating the plant's three-foot-thick cement foundation. It has been estimated that a shockwave of energy traveled through the north part of town in excess of 7,000 miles per hour. That shockwave knocked people to the ground, shattered windows, knocked down walls and doors, lifted roofs off of houses, destroyed vehicles, and caused a devastating amount of damage. The shockwave traveled so fast and with such force that it created a vacuum. As the surrounding atmosphere rushed to fill the vacuum, it caused even more damage. The roofs that had been lifted by the blast were then violently pulled back down, causing them to break rafters and cave in. Ceilings and walls collapsed, and vehicles appeared to implode.

---

2. Texas Governor Greg Abbott, speaking at a community ceremony in West on April 13, 2019 when the Fallen Heroes Memorial was unveiled in the city park.

While the shockwave and the resulting vacuum were tearing things apart, huge pieces of shrapnel and concrete from the plant were hurled through that part of town. Hot metal ignited fires, and other debris caused further damage and injuries. According to the Bureau of Alcohol, Tobacco, and Firearms (ATF), debris was later found up to 2.5 miles away from the plant.

Before the actual explosion, the fire had grown so large that many people came out of their homes to watch it. That small-town curiosity most likely saved lives. The people who were standing outside when the explosion occurred were thrown to the ground or hit by debris, and many were injured in other ways, but they were not trapped inside when their houses were torn apart. Sadly, some of the people who remained indoors did suffer life-long serious injuries, and two of them lost their lives.

One of the firefighters who was battling the inferno at ground zero when the explosion occurred was Robert Payne. Robert is a member of our church, and he is the local funeral director. When the plant exploded, he was literally blown out of his boots. He was thrown about thirty feet into the side of a tank, leaving his boots behind.

The Wines family lived close to the fertilizer plant. Kirk Wines is our church treasurer and one of our local firefighters. When Kirk's wife Pauline and their adult son Brad saw the explosion, they knew Kirk was on the scene and immediately came to the plant to see what they could do to help. Although Brad is not officially a firefighter, he took on the role of a first responder that night and became one of our heroes. Although authorities were warning him to get away from the site, he went in and found Robert lying by the tank where he was unconscious, wounded, and bleeding. Brad picked up Robert and loaded him into the bed of the pickup truck that Pauline was driving. He then found another man who had also been injured and got him into the bed of the truck as well. They took off and got those men to the hospital as quickly as possible. Robert suffered broken ribs, a broken jawbone, shattered teeth, a ruptured ear drum, and a deep shrapnel wound in his arm. His shoulder was mangled, and his ankle was broken, but he survived. Unfortunately, there were some who did not.

That night we lost 15 people. Twelve of those were our first responders who gave their lives fighting for our community.[3] We lost more first responders that night than in any other single event to that date since the attacks on 9/11.

Two people who lived in the nearby apartment complex were killed, and later that evening, we lost a nursing home resident who had a heart attack after being evacuated. West will never forget these 15 people. We will always honor their memory.

- Morris Bridges, West Volunteer Fire Department
- Perry Calvin, Navarro Mills and Mertens Volunteer Fire Departments
- Jerry Chapman, Abbott Volunteer Fire Department
- Cody Dragoo, West Volunteer Fire Department
- Kenneth "Luckey" Harris, Dallas Fire Captain and West resident
- Adolph Lander, resident of West Rest Haven
- Jimmy Matus, honorary firefighter with West Volunteer Fire Department
- Judith Monroe, resident of West Apartments
- Joseph "Joey" Pustejovsky, West Volunteer Fire Department
- Cyrus Reed, Abbott Volunteer Fire Department

---

3. The stories of our firefighters are powerfully portrayed in *The Last Alarm: First Responders' Stories of the West Explosion* by Amber Adamson, 2014 CBM Publishing.

- Mariano C. Saldivar, resident of West Apartments
- Kevin Sanders, Bruceville-Eddy Volunteer Fire Department
- Douglas Snokhous, West Volunteer Fire Department
- Robert Snokhous, West Volunteer Fire Department
- William "Buck" Uptmore Jr., honorary firefighter with West Volunteer Fire Department

It has been estimated that 260 West residents were injured in the explosion. 161 houses were destroyed, and 175 others were damaged. Schools, churches, and small businesses were also damaged or destroyed. That translates to roughly a fourth of the town's structures being destroyed and another fourth being damaged. A thirty-seven square block area of the town's infrastructure was seriously damaged, including water, sewer, and roads.

When the fire broke out at the plant, Dr. George Smith led the effort to evacuate the nursing home because he was aware that an explosion was possible. Dr. Smith, the nursing home staff, and the volunteers were able to get some of the people out of the building before it was destroyed by the blast. When it became clear that they could not get all the residents out in time, they moved some of them to the section farthest from the fertilizer plant and closed the fire doors just before the explosion. Other volunteers came immediately after the blast and joined the efforts to get the rest of the people out. The residents were taken down the street a few blocks to the high school football field. Many other injured people from all over that part of town were taken to the field for triage as well. West EMS Supervisor Tom Marek had been driving a fire truck toward the plant when it blew. He immediately joined Dr. Smith, the other EMTs, medical personnel, and local volunteers at the football field where they were able to render first aid and begin the arduous process of bringing some order to the chaos.

Amid the confusion, a miracle went virtually unnoticed. The explosion had knocked out most of the power in that area. Everything in that neighborhood was dark except the football field. Short of divine intervention, no one can explain why the power stayed on there, but it did. Those lights that usually call our community together on Friday nights in the fall helped our community get through the darkest of nights when we needed them most.

Not long after the triage and treatment began, word spread that the danger had not passed. There was still a tank of about 100 tons of ammonium nitrate and another tank of anhydrous ammonia at ground zero. Either or both of those could blow up next, and that second explosion could be worse than the first. Wisely, the decision was made to move triage from the football field to the community center on the other side of town. Everyone in town who was able to help did so. Nursing home residents and injured people were driven across town in pickup trucks, SUVs, busses, ambulances, and all kinds of emergency vehicles.

That is about the time I arrived at the community center. What I saw when I got there was overwhelming. While it has not been verified, it is widely believed that the number of emergency personnel who were there that night almost matched the total population of West. We have a population of approximately 2,800 and that night there were probably about 2,500 first responders present. People in uniforms were giving and relaying orders, while others were transporting victims, treating the injured, or standing by ready to help when needed. State and county officials were there as well, including McLennan County Emergency Management Coordinator Frank Patterson, who oversaw the response efforts.[4] Eventually, the authorities had to send out a broadcast saying that we could not take any more first responders, so everyone else should just "stand by."

There were injured and frightened people everywhere outside the community center. Some needed help, and others were providing help to those in need. Once all the casualties had been assessed and the nursing home residents had arrived, the big challenge was getting people moved to other nursing facilities and hospitals. There was a steady stream of buses and other vehicles transporting those people to safety. Phil Immicke, Rusty Johnson, and our friend Rick Adams had used our church bus to bring people from the football field, and now they helped transport those folks elsewhere. A nurse who had been driving on the highway when the explosion happened stopped to help and was working with them as well. Everyone who was able was helping those who had been injured or displaced.

I made my way through the massive crowd of busy people to the front door of the community center where the seriously injured were being treated. I explained to the law enforcement officers who were guarding the door that I was a local pastor, and I had come to help. Our local Methodist pastor, Jimmy Sansom, was trying to get in as well, but neither of us of were able to convince the officers to let us through the door. I wanted to go in and pray with the injured and help comfort the people who were scared and hurting. I also assumed that some of the people

---

4. McLennan County Emergency Management Coordinator Frank Patterson not only helped oversee the immediate response the night of the explosion, but he stayed with our community and continued to aid our recovery for the next few years. We are grateful for his dedication and leadership.

in that center had passed away already, and I wanted to make sure their families were not alone. I was told respectfully but firmly that I could not go in. I looked for anyone I could find who was important enough to have a name badge and asked them what I could do to help. None of them knew me, and my title carried no authority in that moment. Today, I understand that they had to do their jobs, and they could not risk letting me, or any other untrained personnel, get in their way. They certainly did the right thing, but being denied the opportunity to help was beyond frustrating. I have never felt so helpless.

As I looked around me, I felt just a little of the anguish that Jeremiah must have felt when he wrote the saddest book of the Bible: Lamentations. Jeremiah survived the destruction of his beloved town of Jerusalem in 586 B.C. when the Babylonians sacked the city and took most of the survivors into captivity. As Jeremiah looked around him at the pain and destruction, he was devastated. He knew that many people had been killed, many more had been injured, and many were still missing. As he mourned, he wrote the book that put words to the unspeakable grief he and his people were experiencing.

At the community center, I had no way of knowing how bad things really were, but like Jeremiah, I knew that people had died, many were injured, and some were still missing. I wanted to do something; I *had* to do something. These were my friends, my church family, the people with whom I had spent two decades building relationships. I had invested most of my adult life in this community, and I had grown to love these people. God had called me to serve this community, and He had created me for that very purpose. Now, all I could do was watch them suffer. I saw a lot of people who were injured and bleeding, many who were crying and shaking in fear, and some who were in shock and did not seem to know where they were. All I could do was walk around and offer encouragement or prayer. When I saw someone crying, I would stop and pray with them. When I saw someone standing alone, I would go to them and visit for a while, offering whatever encouragement I could. Compared to the heroic work of the first responders who had come to town to help us, I felt like I was not able to do much, but I kept at it anyway.

For many hours, I walked around talking and praying and hugging people. It was during that time that Tim Randolph called me. Our church is a part of the Waco Regional Baptist Association, and Tim was the Executive Director of our association. I learned from him how I could get in touch with the Texas Baptist Men.[5] I contacted them and told them that we would need their help. I was assured they would be on their way as soon as possible. Around 3:30 a.m., most of the patients had been transported to area hospitals or nursing facilities, and most of the other people from West had left the scene, so I decided it was time for me to leave as well.

Before I got to the Johnsons' house where my family was staying, Hunter brought Princess there. She had soot all over her feet and apparently could not hear (a condition which passed in a few days). Lisa and Ashley cleaned her up, and the Johnsons prepared a place for her to sleep. Once I finally got there, Lisa and Ashley had already gone to bed, but the whole family was together, and we were safe. I sat down and watched TV for a while. My little, Central Texas town was on *national* news. All the major networks and news stations were introducing West, TX to the world and depicting our nightmare with pictures, videos,

---

5. The "Texas Baptist Men" have since changed their name to "Texans on Mission."

and live shots from helicopters. The announcers were getting experts to guess how many people were injured and how many might have died. As they talked about the casualties, I had the overwhelming sense that I could no longer define reality. It felt as if I had entered a new dimension, and nothing would ever again be as I had known it. I turned off the TV and sat in the living room praying. I was pleading with God to help me make sense of it all. I did not sleep at all that night. There were only a couple of hours left until sunrise, and I just sat there thinking about the pain, the sorrow, the loss, and the fear. Twelve hours earlier, we were cheering for Ashley as she ran across the finish line. Now, not only had our family changed, but our whole world had changed forever.

I kept wondering how many people had died, what had happened to all the nursing home residents who had to be relocated, how many homes were lost, and how we would ever recover. Eventually, I thought about my own home. I knew most of our windows and doors were missing, and the roof had been badly damaged, so I wondered if the contents would be safe overnight. That was just about the time it began to rain.

The Next Day

The next morning, I went to the church, not knowing if I would even be allowed to get to it. Most of the north side of town had been cordoned off; no one could go past Virginia Street. Those restrictions were put into place to protect our safety, but also to protect the evidence in the area that was being treated like a very large crime scene. At that time, no one knew the cause of the explosion, the extent of the damage, or the number of casualties. Local, county, state, and federal officials were working together to complete their search and rescue efforts and to begin trying to determine what had happened.

Our church sits on the corner of N. Marable and W. Virginia. That meant the building was just inside the area that had been cordoned off. The door that we all use during the week faces W. Virginia St., so I hoped that I might be able to use that door since it was directly on the border. When I arrived, I talked with the state law enforcement officer who was nearby. His job that morning was to watch the border and make sure no one entered the area that was off limits. I showed him we were only feet from the door, and he agreed that we could use that entrance, but we were not to exit from any of the other doors, and we could not walk around outside the building. We also agreed that we would not hold any congregational meetings there because we would not be able to keep people on the right side of the boundary.

I was still in shock and grief, so my memory of that time is a bit foggy, but I do remember that Dr. David Hardage, who was the Executive Director of the Baptist General Convention of Texas, met me at the church that morning with some of the other denominational leaders. They supported me, encouraged me, and prayed for me. Their presence and their prayers helped comfort some of my fears, and I felt like I was beginning to breathe again. On behalf of the BGCT, Dr. Hardage gave me some cash. He and his team already knew what I had not yet realized. I lived about a half mile from the fertilizer plant, and there was no way I was going to be able to get to my house anytime soon. That meant I had no clothes, no food, and no toiletries or medications. I was still wearing the clothes I had put on the morning of the previous day because that was all I had. Overnight I had become homeless and could not get to anything that I needed. I gratefully received the cash, and we lived off it for a while.

Tim Randolph from the Waco Regional Baptist Association also came to the church that morning. I told Tim I didn't know what to do. I was aware that I was not thinking straight yet, and I had no idea what to do next, much less how to lead people through something like this. He prayed with me and assured me that he and the association would be there to help us get through it. True to his word, he became a good friend on whom I could depend. He connected us with all kinds of helpful resources and introduced us to several people who helped us throughout our recovery.

Later that day, there was an impromptu gathering at the community center. I was asked to come and pray with the people who were there. When I arrived at the parking lot, I found dozens of people who had come together to comfort one another. I had to fight back my emotions when I saw my daughter, Ashley, and a group of her friends crying in one big group hug. We had known some of those girls their whole lives. While I was brokenhearted for them, I was also encouraged by the fact that they did have each other. In the parking lot of the community center, I led the group in prayer. That was just the first of numerous times I would be able to pray with the community about our losses and our eventual recovery.

That afternoon, I was in an informal gathering of some of the leaders in our community. The only part of that meeting that I remember is when our mayor, Tommy Muska, entered the room and sat down exhausted. He said something I have never forgotten, although I did not understand it at the time. He said, "We got all our boys. We got them all." The first responders and officials who were working in the north part of town were still in search and recovery mode. I had not heard any reliable reports on casualties. The experts on the national news the night before were estimating horrific numbers, but I had not yet heard anything reliable. When Mayor Muska said, "We got all our boys," I interpreted that to mean that we had some children who had been missing but had finally been found. Later, when I learned more about what had happened, I realized he was talking about his friends, his "brothers," in the fire department who did not survive. Brave firefighters from all over central Texas not only continued working through the night to get the multiple fires under control after the explosion, but they also dug through the rubble to recover our fallen heroes. Firefighters often remind each other, "Two go in and two come out." It is a statement that inspires courage because it is a promise that no firefighter will have to enter the flames alone, and no firefighter will be left behind. In keeping with that tradition, an honor guard stood at attention at the explosion site until all the remains had been found and recovered. Then, firefighters from the surrounding areas joined the remaining firefighters from West and formed a large honor guard who solemnly and respectfully ushered our fallen heroes out of the smoldering debris and ash across the street to the high school parking lot where vehicles were waiting to take them away. From the moment the first honor guard took his position at the site until they were laid to rest, none of the twelve were ever left alone. Someone dressed in full uniform and standing at attention watched over them day and night. "Two go in and two come out," no matter what.

CHAPTER 2
SCIENCE FICTION OR REALITY?

"The world is indeed full of peril, and in it there are many dark places; but still there is much that is fair, and though in all lands love is now mingled with grief, it grows perhaps the greater."
J.R.R. Tolkien [1]

"It's surreal." That phrase is often heard after a disaster. As those affected look around them and see the devastation, the anguish on the faces of their neighbors, and a landscape that looks nothing like it did the day before, the experience is frightening and disorienting. It feels like wandering through a science fiction movie. Nothing seems real. There is a lingering anticipation that the world might somehow return to normal, as if waking from a nightmare, but at the same time, there is the heartbreaking acknowledgement that this is indeed reality, and there is no easy escape from it. For those first few days after the explosion, we tried to encourage one another, but each of us was dealing with great pain, loss, anxiety, and fear. We carried that with us as we moved from one gathering to the next, doing our part to hold things together while inside we were falling apart.

---

1.   J. R. R. Tolkien, The Fellowship of the Ring, (Allen & Unwin, 1954).

Those days of wandering through a misty haze of horror so unsettling that our minds could not fully comprehend our reality will always remain in my memory. It is an experience that I hope to never live through again. Since I have lived through it and have subsequently walked through it with others, I have learned some important lessons that might be helpful to leaders who must face similar experiences. Here are some practical ways in which a minister can respond to an immediate crisis and be most helpful in the early hours and days after a disaster.

The Ministry of Presence

During that darkest night, I learned that sometimes there are no words. When we minister to those who are in crisis, we often struggle to find the "right" words to say. The truth is, when the person you are helping gets through the shock and their mind begins to clear, they will not remember anything you said in the moment of crisis anyway. What they will remember is you were there with them.

Throughout scripture, God cares for His people by reminding them that He is with them. His presence comforts them even in the darkest of valleys (Psalm 23:4). He never promises a cessation of life's problems or protection from the heartaches of a fallen world, but He does promise to be *with us*. We therefore cannot make light of the ministry of presence. It is our pride that drives us to say the "right" thing. We err when we expect that we should be able to say something to make the situation better. Let your compassion override your pride and just be there. Let go of the unrealistic expectations that you feel in the moment of crisis and just be present. Be with the person who is struggling, and let your presence reassure them that they are not alone.

In the Sermon on the Mount, Jesus declared that His people were salt and light to the world around us (Matthew 5:13–16). Salt can neither enhance nor preserve meat unless it actually comes into contact with the meat. Light can have no effect unless it enters the place of darkness. There is something sacred about showing up.

There are three major components to the ministry of presence, none of which come naturally to most leaders. The first is **listen**. Instead of accepting the undue responsibility of determining what to say, accept your role in doing the harder task of listening. Listen actively with eye contact, sincere compassion, and a caring, non-judgmental expression on your face. In other words, listen with your heart as much as with your ears. Stay focused on the person who is speaking instead of thinking about what you "should" say next. While it is always good guidance, James' instruction is particularly important to the ministry of presence, "…be quick to hear, slow to speak" (1:19). There will be an abundance of opportunity to speak words of encouragement and comfort later, but these moments are not intended for conversation. Just listen. Proverbs reminds us, "If one gives an answer before he hears, it is his folly and shame" (18:13). In times of crisis, the need for personal connection outweighs the need for profound inspiration. Your primary objective at that time is to provide a safe, healing experience for a person who is afraid and in pain. Never express shock at anything the hurting person says. Your shocked reaction can become a snapshot in the other person's mind that stays with them, carrying with it feelings of guilt or shame that can hinder their healing.

Another key component to the ministry of presence is **silence.** Not only do you want to avoid the temptation to talk while the other person is processing their pain, but there will also be times when you need to be quiet even when they are not speaking. This is uncomfortable for many leaders because we feel an obligation to fill the emptiness with words of wisdom or hopeful phrases that will lighten the other's burden. The wisdom of Proverbs is helpful again: "When words are many, transgression is not lacking, but whoever restrains his lips is prudent" (10:19). In the earliest moments of crisis, the person with whom you are ministering needs time for fear to subside so their defenses can come down and allow their mind to catch up to reality. That takes time. At first, they cannot think clearly, much less manage their emotional responses. Sometimes the most compassionate thing you can say is nothing at all. Just let the silence be. It is in that safe, comforting silence that the hurting person can begin to process what has happened. You do not need to create silence or force it, but when it happens, learn to embrace it. Your ministry in that moment is simply being present.

Which brings us to what may be the most difficult component for leaders to utilize. While you listen and while you sit in silence, you will have to **wait.** Waiting is a challenge for leaders because we want to solve problems and tell people how to move forward. We want to move; we want to act. Leadership is taking people from one experience to the next, so it can be challenging for a leader to wait. Work against the temptation to move on too quickly. Avoid checking the time, do not look around for the next person in need, just wait. It may feel like it is taking a long time, but if you are present in the moment, it does not really take that long for the person to benefit from your presence. The important thing is that you are not just in the same vicinity but that you are actually present. That is, you are tuned in to anything they want to say, and you are listening actively, letting silence bring healing while being so attentive that the person in need is assured that you are indeed with them in that moment. One of the verses that made all the difference to us in our crisis was Psalm 46:1, in which we were reminded that God is "very present" in times of trouble. Let that be your goal in those early frightening moments of despair. Go beyond being in the right place at the right time and be very present to the person who needs to know they are not alone in the darkness.

Sometimes all you can do is sit on the curb next to someone who is crying and cry with them. Sometimes all you can do is give a hug to a neighbor. When those times come, rest assured you are providing a valuable service and conducting a meaningful ministry. When it's time to get up from the curb or release the hug, silently whisper a prayer that your friend will continue to experience God's presence even as you say goodbye.

In the First Twenty-Four Hours

Immediately after the disaster, the people in your community will feel confused, disoriented, and afraid as they see the results of the event that has changed their world. Their emotions will be difficult to regulate, their perceptions will be skewed, and their ability to determine next steps will be drastically impaired. The same things will most likely be true for you, but as a leader, you can guide your people through those first hours and provide them with some assurance that there is a way through the confusion.

As soon as you can catch your breath, start thinking about the most important steps to take within the first twenty-four hours. That begins with a personal assessment of your own loss. Are you and your family safe? Do you and your family have the necessary shelter, food, and clothing to get through the next forty-eight hours? If your personal needs can be met sufficiently for a couple of days at least, you can resume your role of leadership as soon as possible.

You will need to focus on four areas of concern as soon as you are able to do so. First, evaluate (to the best of your ability) the safety of your facilities. Particularly if you lead a church, people will soon begin turning to you for shelter and assistance. You need to know if your building is available as a safe place for people to gather and seek help. You also need to make sure that you, the staff, and other volunteers have safe places in which to work. Repairs and cleanup procedures can happen later. At first, you just need to know if you and the people with whom you work can use your facilities safely or if you need to make other arrangements.

Second, you will want to establish communication with your people. In many ways, that is easier today than it was for us over a decade ago. Since everyone has a cell phone and most people connect with others on at least one social media platform, you have a good chance of being able to reach people relatively quickly. However, all that communication is dependent upon cellular and/or internet service. Those may not be available to you, so you will have to find other means of communication. Even if it is difficult to do, make communication a priority in those first hours after the disaster. Your people need to know you are alright and will be able to help them. They need to know the status of their friends and loved ones in your church or organization. They also need to know what to do next. Amid the surreal science fiction haze all around them, they need to know there is a path to something stable. By communicating effectively and early, you can help them find their way to a renewed sense of security.

As soon as possible, find ways to communicate with your people, but do not assume the responsibility of doing all the communicating. Involve others as much as possible. This will not only make your communication efforts more efficient, but it will give your staff and volunteers something meaningful to do, thus facilitating their return to reality as well. Have small group leaders get in touch with the members of their groups. Have ministry leaders connect with their ministry participants. Ask Bible study leaders to connect with the people in their classes. Your goal at this point is not to communicate a lot of information but to establish lines of communication and begin finding out who survived, who is injured, and who is missing. Once those lines of communication are established, you can begin finding out more about the needs of the people you serve and making plans for next steps, but all of that will come later. In this earliest stage, you just need to get people talking and let them know how they can reach you. Opening those lines of communication will prove invaluable and should be considered a top priority for day one of your recovery.

The third priority for your immediate response is to organize your decision makers. There will be an overwhelming number of decisions to make in the very near future, and you need to determine as soon as possible who will be involved in making those decisions. In West, our school board and city council each held emergency meetings as soon as the sun rose after the explosion. I gathered the deacons of our church later that day. Every church has its own polity and decision-making process so figure out what works best in your setting and plan on getting in touch with those people as soon as possible. Just like every church is unique so is every disaster, so it may not be feasible for you to gather your decision-makers in the first twenty-fours, but you will at least want to make your plans in that time. Determine when and where you can get together or meet via video conference. When you inform them about the meeting plans, ask them to keep praying and to begin thinking about what needs to be handled, but remind them you have no answers yet. This early meeting is not like a normal board meeting in which you can inform the decision-makers about what is happening in your organization. The purpose of this meeting is to start thinking together and sharing responsibility for determining the best ways to help people begin their recovery. You may not even leave that first meeting with a plan, but you will have initiated an essential conversation.

Finally, you will want to be making plans for your church or organization to continue to meet. I list this last because it is not as urgent as the other three, but I also include it in the list of things to do in the first twenty-four hours because it has great significance, and it will be important for you to make those plans as quickly as possible. Word will soon spread throughout your church family or organization about who was lost or injured and how bad the situation is for some families. People will grieve the losses they hear about and will be relieved to hear about friends and neighbors who survived. No matter how much it helps the people to hear about those they love, they need to see their friends in person. Hugs, handshakes, and shoulders for tears are necessary for people to begin accepting the reality in which they now live. Your people need to be together as soon as they can. Even if you cannot get to your facilities, make plans to meet again at your regular time as soon as possible. This is especially important for churches, for the reasons discussed in the next chapter. Even amid the chaos and confusion surrounding people who have survived a disaster, a gathering of their community can serve as a promise that life will eventually feel real again.

CHAPTER 3
GOD IS BIGGER
THAN ALL OF THIS

"God is our refuge and strength, a very present help in trouble."
Psalm 46:1

The explosion in West occurred on the north side of town. That entire area was immediately cordoned off and access to that part of town was restricted to official personnel while county, state, and federal officials tried to determine what happened. Our church was barely inside that cordoned off area for the first few days. Our parking lot on the south side of the street was accessible, but the building on the north side of the street was not. Our staff got permission to enter the building from the south end so we could get started on our recovery efforts, but we could not hold gatherings in the building.

The day after the explosion was a Thursday. I started getting calls and emails that morning asking if we were going to be able to have worship on Sunday. I responded to each message that yes, we would have worship, I just did not know how or where. We were committed to meeting that Sunday morning for three reasons.

First, while we had been in contact with everyone in one way or another, we had not yet been able to see each other, and we knew that physical contact would be important. Second, we knew the church is a family, and family needs to be together in times of crisis. Third, and most important, we knew this was an opportunity to demonstrate that God is worthy of our worship regardless of our circumstances. No matter what we are going through, God never changes. God deserves our worship when things are going well and when our world is falling apart. Our circumstances do not change God's character, and it was important to us that we begin our journey of recovery with this act of faith.

The deacons helped me think through all our options and come up with a plan. We started implementing that plan immediately. Our community has an annual festival called "WestFest" in which we celebrate the town's Czech heritage and culture. West-Fest owns a field on the south end of town that is used for parking during the festival. We asked them if we could borrow that field for worship on Sunday, and they enthusiastically agreed. We had only a couple of days to make all the necessary plans and handle the logistics for an outdoor worship service, which is something none of us had ever undertaken.

We were able to get a party company out of nearby Waco to bring folding chairs and set them up for us. We had intended to pay rent on the chairs, but the company considered it a donation and didn't charge anything. One of the deacons is an electrician, so he made sure we had power. Another deacon has a flatbed trailer, so he hauled that over and set it up in front of the chairs. The good people at Columbus Avenue Baptist Church loaned us a sound system, and one of their sound techs volunteered to set it up and run it for us.

That Sunday morning, we could not meet at our church, but we still met as a family for worship. As it was the first time many of us had seen each other, there were many hugs and many tears. The national media was there because they had come to town soon after the explosion and knew about our outdoor worship service. That unique service is one that none of us will ever forget. A flatbed trailer became our altar, folding chairs became our pews, the outdoors became our sanctuary, and a grassy field became holy ground. God met us there. With news cameras surrounding us and a world watching as our witness, we worshiped Him with everything we had left in us. Like the psalmist, in our distress and anguish, we cried out to the Lord (Psalm 118:5), and to God be the glory, He moved among us. He restored our strength, eased our fear, began healing our pain, and gave us hope. Thursday through Saturday were days of pain, confusion, sorrow, and suffering, but on Sunday, God started changing things. On Sunday, God started changing us!

As a part of that life-giving worship service, we read from Psalm 46:1, "God is our refuge and strength, a very present help in trouble." Drawing from the power of that verse, I reassured our community that although the devastation and loss all around us was terrible, "God is bigger than all of this." The media coverage was extensive, and the story even reached the president of the United States. President Barack Obama quoted our theme later in a national memorial service in honor of our fallen first responders. He talked about our outdoor worship service, and he reminded the audience three times, "God is bigger than all of this."

That Sunday morning in the field initiated our forward progress, defined us as a people, and shaped our entire recovery. We headed into the most difficult years in our church's long history with the courage that can only come from faith, and we did so together. We began the hard work of recovery as a united family.

I share that story to emphasize the importance of leading your church or organization to continue worshiping and serving even in the most difficult of times. They can face hard times better if they know their God is able to see them through. We can help them know that if we stress to them that God is still God, and He is always worthy of our worship. Since His character does not change, His worthiness does not change. Our word "worship" comes from an old English word, "weorthscipe," which meant worth-ship. We worship because God is inherently worthy of our praise. A few years ago, Pastor Gary Hamrick preached a sermon in which he taught his congregation to say, "When I don't understand God's ways, I have to cling to God's worth—that He is good even when times aren't."[1] Even in Job's suffering and loss he declared, "Naked I came from my mother's womb, and naked shall I return. The LORD gave, and the LORD has taken away; blessed be the name of the LORD" (Job 1:21). Whether he lived in a time of great blessing or suffered through a time of great loss, Job knew that God deserved his worship. By keeping worship a priority throughout your recovery, you are declaring the truth that God is big enough to trust, and by doing that, you are encouraging your people with the faith they need to survive and thrive.

There is another reason that gathering for worship is essential during the most difficult times. The goal of worship is to focus on God. At our church, we have five guiding principles we call "plumb lines." One of those plumb lines states, "Worship is what

---

1.   Gary Hamrick in his sermon "Miracle at the Pool," Cornerstone Chapel in Leesburg, VA, June 5, 2022.

we do for God, not what the church does for us." In genuine worship, we focus on the Lord. If our focus is on God, it is not on ourselves. Leading your people into sincere worship allows them to change their perspective. They are able to look beyond their pain and suffering and see the God who is bigger than all of that. Sometimes we still sing an old chorus that reminds us to "Turn your eyes upon Jesus. Look full in His wonderful face. And the things of earth will grow strangely dim in the light of His glory and grace."[2]

In a practical sense, meeting together soon after a tragic event may be the first experience your people have that is familiar. Since the tragedy, their lives will have been full of chaos, uncertainty, confusion, and fear. Giving them a familiar experience can serve as an anchor that holds them steady. For that reason, it is a good idea to meet in the same place if you can or at least at the scheduled time when your people are used to meeting. That familiarity can bring much needed peace that quickly translates into hope.

"God is Bigger Than All of This" became our theme during the short-term relief phase of our recovery.[3] That kind of reminder to continue worshiping God and trusting God to get us through hard times is essential to navigating the relief phase. Your people need to be reminded that God has not changed, even though their world has, and God will see them through what they are currently facing. Psalm 34:18–19 encourages us to remain faithful, "The LORD is near to the brokenhearted and saves the crushed in spirit. Many are the afflictions of the righteous, but the LORD delivers him out of them all."

---

2.   Aaron Shust and Paul Baloche, "Turn Your Eyes Upon Jesus,"; Bridge Building Music, Inc., CP Shust Tunes, Integrity Worship Music, Lead Worship Songs, ©2016.

3.   More will be presented about the phases of recovery in subsequent chapters.

CHAPTER 4
SPIRITUAL LEADERSHIP IN TIMES OF CRISIS

"God whispers to us in our pleasures, speaks in our conscience, but shouts in our pain: it is his megaphone to rouse a deaf world."
C. S. Lewis [1]

Leading well is never simple, but leading people through crisis and recovery can be particularly difficult. It involves unusual levels of hard work, personal sacrifice, vigilance, self-awareness, time management, and communication. It requires so much energy and attention that it can be draining to the point of exhaustion very quickly. This is particularly true if the leader has been personally affected by the disaster and is trying to manage their own recovery, as well as caring for the community. It is essential that the leader spends time in honest, regular self-evaluation and self-care. Amid the chaos, pain, and suffering of others, that kind of attention on oneself might feel counterproductive and perhaps even unethical. During times of crisis, however, the leader must recognize that paying attention to his own personal health and wellbeing is not selfish; it is mandatory if the leader is going to be

1.   C. S. Lewis, *The Problem of Pain*, (New York, The Macmillan Company 1944).

properly equipped to help the most people in the most effective ways. A leader who ignores her own needs will not be able to meet the needs of others for long.

If a leader only thinks of themselves while others are struggling, there is certainly a problem, but the committed leader's goal in self-evaluation and self-care is the ultimate well-being of those in his care. When balancing these priorities, I have found it helpful to consider Jesus' words in Luke 10:27: "You shall love the Lord your God with all your heart and with all your soul and with all your strength and with all your mind, and your neighbor as yourself." Using that verse as a guide, ministers can learn to check on themselves and then check on others.

Check In with Yourself

When struggling through complex issues, dealing with difficult people, navigating personal loss, and leading others into recovery, a leader must check in with herself from time to time to make sure she is able to lead in meaningful and healthy ways. That self-evaluation begins with the instruction from Luke 10:27[2] to love the Lord your God with all your heart, mind, soul, and strength. The words "heart," "soul," "mind," and "strength" enable us to do some self-evaluation into our emotional, spiritual, physical, and mental well-being. Admittedly, the original hearers of those words did not associate the terms exactly as we do today, but they can be helpful for us, nonetheless. For example, when we hear the word "heart," we think of the seat of our emotions. When the people listening to Jesus heard Him refer to the "heart,"

---

2.   This verse contains the essence of the Old Testament law included in Deuteronomy 6:5 and Leviticus 19:18. A version of this teaching appears in all three synoptic gospels: Matthew 22:37–39, Mark 12:30–31, and Luke 10:27.

they knew that to mean the center of oneself, including emotions, thoughts, will, and spirituality. For our purposes, we will apply the words almost like a mnemonic device and refer to them in the ways we usually use them today.

As you lead through difficult times, regularly ask yourself, "Am I currently able to love the Lord with my whole heart?" Let your answer to that question help you evaluate how you are doing emotionally. Then ask, "Am I currently able to love God with all my soul?" This helps you focus on your spiritual well-being. Asking, "Am I able to love God with all my mind right now?" will help you evaluate your mental status, particularly your ability to focus. Finally, you can evaluate your physical health by asking, "Can I use all of my normal strength to love God right now?"

Struggling in any of these areas is not a sign of sin or unreasonable weakness, especially during a crisis. There is no expectation that you should be able to avoid emotional conflicts, spiritual uncertainties, mental distractions, or physical exhaustion. The goal of this exercise is not to produce guilt but to conduct an honest evaluation of how you are doing at any given moment. You can check in with yourself and track your personal health over time.

Emotional Well-Being

To enhance and protect your emotional well-being, stay in touch with a friend who is not involved in the disaster. When you are surrounded by heartache, frustration, pain, and sorrow, it can be difficult to maintain a realistic and healthy perspective. Having a trusted friend who is not in the fray can provide an anchor to reality that can be quite helpful. That friend can also offer the encouragement and support that leaders do not usually receive from the people to whom they are ministering. In addition to that friend, make a conscious effort to stay connected to your family. You need them and they need you, but it is too easy to take them for granted and neglect them when you are already feeling pulled in so many different directions.

Spiritual Well-Being

To protect and enhance your spiritual health, make certain that you do not neglect your time with God. Our time with God is often one of the first things we set aside when our schedules become too full. In the heights of crisis management, it might seem that time with God can wait because if anybody understands what you are going through, it is God. We know that God is merciful and knows all about our situation already, so why not get on to more important things for now? The truth is, there are not more important things, and you cannot adequately face the challenges of a hectic day without the spiritual experience of being in God's presence.

Because time with God is so important, we found it meaningful and beneficial to begin each day with a prayer time for all the volunteers who were in town to help us in our recovery. We met early each morning and invited community members and volunteers to join us for prayer. If you do something like this, I suggest that you avoid the temptation to make it a Bible study or teaching time. Just start the day in prayer. Also, do everything possible to avoid canceling your regular church services. Your spiritual well-being and that of your people is too important to put worship on the back burner. Finally, you can strengthen the faith of your people if you consistently remind them that God is present and is at work among them. If you use every opportunity to encourage others with that reminder, it will encourage you as well. We used the phrases, "God is bigger than all of this" and "God is good, and West is blessed." However, you choose to say it, say it often. You and your people need to know that the "very present help in trouble" (Psalm 46:1) is at work and will see them through.

Physical Well-Being

After our outdoor worship service on the Sunday following the explosion, we went to have lunch with some friends. As I ate my lunch, I realized it was the first real meal I had eaten since we had dinner the previous Wednesday evening. Thursday through Saturday were so overwhelming and everything was such a blur that I had lost my appetite and had not eaten much of anything in all that time. I also had not slept well any of those nights. From that experience, I learned the importance of paying attention to my own physical health. Even if you have no appetite and you are constantly on the run from crisis to meeting to press conference to problem solving to person in need, make sure you eat. Your body may not tell you that you are hungry but make sure that you stay fueled and adequately hydrated. For the first few days after the disaster, this may take more of a conscious effort than you are accustomed to giving it.

In a similar way, get plenty of rest. Since I could not sleep, I made the mistake of staying busy and working when I should have been resting. Even if sleep does not come, lay down on a regular schedule and rest. Even though adrenaline is making you feel energetic, you are expending more energy than normal, and your body needs to recharge. In 1 Kings 19, Elijah faced a disaster of sorts. He was in fear for his life. His stress level was through the roof. He was depressed and ready to give up. God ministered to him by helping him sleep and eat. The fact that God used those remedies to restore Elijah speaks volumes to how we can care for ourselves during stressful times.

Mental Well-Being

Consider what it means to love God with all your mind. While the terms are often used interchangeably, I take emotional health and mental health to mean different things. Mental health in this context refers to our ability to use our minds effectively. In the early days of disaster relief and recovery, most people report various levels of confusion. Suddenly, their world no longer makes any sense. I found it difficult to concentrate and difficult to remember the information that I needed to process each day.

You can take some simple steps to support your mental abilities when life is too much. First, write everything down. Even if you normally have a good memory, that memory cannot be trusted in times of crisis. Let your phone be your brain. In addition to regular means of communication, you can use your phone to write notes, give yourself reminders, manage your calendar, set alarms and timers, leave yourself voice memos, and a multitude of other functions that you might normally depend on your brain to accomplish. Do not be dismayed by distractions and confusion; expect them. You will experience them to some degree. You can minimize their effects, however, by writing everything down and utilizing your phone to help you think more clearly.

Another way to care for your mental well-being is to depend on trusted advisors. Ask the people you trust for advice and lean on them heavily. They are probably able to see things more clearly and think more effectively than you can on your own. Proverbs

11:14 teaches us, "Where there is no guidance, a people falls, but in an abundance of counselors there is safety." In a similar way, Proverbs 19:20 instructs us to, "Listen to advice and accept instruction, that you may gain wisdom in the future."

Check In with Others

The last part of Luke 10:27 turns our attention to others: "and your neighbor as yourself." Again, we are using the verse as a mnemonic device. Since this verse is so familiar, you can remember it and think of it often as you deal with all the frantic work of bringing organization into chaos. As you use the first part of the verse to think through various ways to check in with yourself and evaluate your own well-being, you can begin to let the last part of the verse remind you to check in with others. You can love your neighbor in a variety of ways, but I want to suggest some that are specific to disaster recovery. Let us consider them based on three kinds of relationships that are meaningful. Each one narrows the scope a little as you focus on your community, your church, and your family.

Community

First, as you are tracking your own well-being by using the first part of our verse, you want to begin tracking the overall well-being of your community as well. In Chapter 6, I will describe a chart that can be used to track your community's emotional response. Although every community is unique and every disaster is unique, there is a somewhat predictable sequence of emotional responses that your community will experience as they progress through recovery. When you become familiar with that process, it will help you understand what members of your community are experiencing, and you will be better equipped to help them move toward resolution.

In addition to tracking your community's progress, find out if a local VOAD has been established. VOAD stands for Voluntary Organizations Active in Disasters. There are state and national VOADs, but often communities that experience disasters form their own local VOAD. This group includes the various disaster response teams, volunteer organizations, charitable groups, non-profits, foundations, etc., who are working together to assist the community's recovery. Through regular meetings and consistent communication, the groups work together to coordinate their efforts. If your community forms a VOAD, ask to be included so you can represent your church or organization in cooperation with the other entities who are committed to recovery efforts.

You can also serve the people in your community by opening your facility to volunteers. If they are just there for a day, let them use your facility to organize their group or meet for meals and breaks. Provide overnight shelter for them if need be. We had volunteers sleeping in our Sunday School rooms for months. You may even be able to help coordinate the work of those volunteers. With the help of a team from the Texas Baptists,[3] we were able to receive assistance requests from our neighbors who had been affected and pair them up with volunteers who had come to help. It is not uncommon for a local church to assume that role during recovery. Our associate pastor, Phil Immicke, did a marvelous job doing this for us. He coordinated which volunteers were coming when, categorized the needs of our residents, and connected those who could help with those in need. Our church became a major

---

3.   Formally, Baptist General Convention of Texas.

hub of activity during our recovery. We served as the headquarters for multiple volunteer organizations but primarily the Texas Baptist Men (now called Texans on Mission). They stayed with us for many months. They fed survivors and volunteers three meals a day, provided laundry services and shower facilities, made chaplains available, helped with countless repairs and cleanup projects, and even helped with most of our demolitions. The work these hard-working servants do for communities in crisis is invaluable, and the efficacy of their service is immeasurable. West could not have recovered without their help.

You may also choose to provide space in your facility for donated items but be careful because that can quickly become overwhelming. You can be inundated with old hand-me-downs and garage sale junk that people "donate" to help the "victims." If someone in your church is willing to undertake it, though, being a clearing house for usable donated items can be a meaningful ministry. If you have some volunteers who can organize and distribute the donated items, that is a good way to manage resources and get people what they need.

Whether your community has a VOAD or not, be sure that you stay in touch and cooperate with other local leaders. When we were well into our recovery efforts, we realized that our community lacked a central forum for communication among leaders. The Kiwanis Club did its thing, the City Council did its thing, the School District did its thing, etc. We were not coordinating our work and leading our community cooperatively. Ben Younger was a wise man who befriended many of the leaders in West and brought us together on a regular basis so we could communicate and work together. If your community does not have a way for leaders to meet and work together, you may need to be "Ben" for your community and make that happen.

The people in your community will quickly become frustrated, as FEMA, insurance, and mortgage companies require a great deal of complicated paperwork. You can love your neighbor by helping them understand how to fill out the forms they need for FEMA, how to deal with insurance, and what to expect from their mortgage companies. I will share more about these topics in Chapter 8, but for now, let me suggest that you find a church member or friend who can help people with paperwork and become the connection between the person with questions and the one who can help them find answers. The ministry of referral is valuable and even essential at times. Find someone who is willing to help with clerical issues, and be ready to refer people who need that kind of help.

Let your community know how your church or organization is prepared to help. This not only lets the affected members of your community know where they can turn for assistance, but it also establishes your church or organization as a group of people who care and are willing to respond. Your community will re-member your people for their compassionate service for many years to come, which means you will have more opportunities in the future to do Kingdom work and to bring glory to God.

Church

As a leader in your church, you already love your people. When disaster strikes and you see them hurting yet serving one another, your love for them increases exponentially. A major part of loving your neighbor through disaster recovery is caring for your own church family. One way to do that is to let them know how they can communicate with you and with one another. Normal means of communication may not be available, and their opportunities to see each other will probably be limited, so help them know how to stay in touch.

You are going to be carrying too much responsibility and will have too many things on your mind to be able to handle everything that needs to get done. You probably will not be able to effectively manage all your regular duties and all the recovery-related work and still deal with your own personal recovery. One of the most important moves you can make to show love for your church is to hand off some responsibility. Lean on your decision-making body, whether that is deacons, a council, a board, or elders. We appointed a small committee of three trustees just to handle the funds that were being donated to the church. That group was responsible for receiving requests for assistance and distributing the funds. We had another small group of retired teachers who wrote thank you notes all day to donors and volunteers. Depending on others to take on some of those jobs not only makes it easier for you to handle other tasks, but it also gives people a way to serve. Many of the people in your church will welcome opportunities to help because it makes them feel needed, and it helps them make progress in their own recovery.

Love your church family enough to let down your guard and be transparent. Do not pretend to have the answers or to be so spiritual that you are unaffected by the losses you have suffered. Your people need you to walk through this experience with them, not just to direct them on how to get through it on their own. My father was a biology professor at Baylor University until he died from multiple myeloma at the age of 44. After his diagnosis, he told his students he was dying, but since they were Biology students and he was their professor, he offered them a unique opportunity. He told his students that he was still their teacher and would teach them until the end. If any of them wanted to walk through his final days with him, he would answer their questions and share his experiences so they could learn what happens when a person with a terminal diagnosis faces death. Many years later, one of his students wrote my family a note expressing how much that meant to him. My dad taught with transparency, and he shared his journey with his students until that journey ended.

As a Christian leader, your people need to know you are real, and they need you to join them in the struggle and walk down the road of recovery alongside them. Do not hide your pain and sorrow. Feel free to express your concerns and your struggles. Because of the love you share for one another, you can face this turmoil together.

Family

Remember that some of the neighbors you are to love may live in your own home. When you think about people you want to check in with from time to time, do not neglect those closest to you. During times of crisis and recovery, a leader's family see the heavy weight of responsibility the leader carries, and they recognize the stress the leader is under. They can see it in your dulled eyes, your slower gait, your tense facial expressions, your downturned gaze, and your sullen demeanor. As leaders, we often stand up straight and tall when we are out and about, bravely shouldering all the responsibilities that come with leadership. We are careful with our words and deliberate in our actions. But then we go home. When we get home, we tend to let down our guard, relax our stiff upper lip, and release our frustrations. Unfortunately, that release is often directed toward the people we love because we know we are safe around them. They will love us regardless, so we unload all the negative stuff that we have had to secretly carry all day. Despite our exhaustion and our natural tendency to relax at home, leaders must always make an intentional effort to show love to our families.

One of the reasons that effort must be intentional is because when our family members see our struggles, they want to reduce our stress, so they often choose not to ask questions or ask for help. They want to make things easier instead of making them harder. Since the leader is finally able to rest and for the first time all day, no one is asking questions or requesting help, it becomes far too easy for the leader to neglect their family. Since their family members are not voicing any needs, leaders may feel like they can finally relax and not have to deal with anyone else's problems for a while. The sad irony is that when that happens, the people who need us most get the least from us.

Avoid the all-too-common tendencies to take your family for granted or take your frustrations out on them. Be aware that those tendencies exist, and decide early on that you are going to be vigilant in watching for them and avoiding them. As soon as you are physically and emotionally able, take specific steps to let your family know that the other people affected by the disaster are not any more important than they are. Tell them and show them that they are still your priority and always will be. Ask about their needs, especially if they are trying to protect you by not sharing them freely.

Spiritual leadership is never easy, but it is particularly challenging during disaster and recovery. Remember the verse that we can use as a mnemonic device to help us check in with ourselves and with others. Even when things are tough, "'Love the Lord your God with all your heart and with all your soul and with all your strength and with all your mind'; and, 'Love your neighbor as yourself'" (Luke 10:27 NIV).

CHAPTER 5
THE KEY TO
UNDERSTANDING
DISASTER RECOVERY

"For everything there is a season, and a time for every matter under heaven." Ecclesiastes 3:1

Most of the confusion and much of the conflict that surrounds disaster recovery can be mitigated if we understand the structure of recovery. It is not just one long journey. Disaster recovery occurs in phases. Each phase serves different purposes and requires different responses. While each disaster is unique there are at least three phases in every recovery: rescue, relief, recovery.[1]

The **rescue phase** is the shortest of the three. In that initial phase, first responders and emergency management officials react. People who are lost or trapped are rescued. Those who are injured are treated or transported to medical facilities. The remains of the deceased are recovered, and the next of kin are notified. The casualties and fatalities are meticulously recorded and reported

---

1.   Some models include a preparation phase before the disaster event and a mitigation phase at the end of the recovery process. For the purposes of this book, the three main phases described are sufficient to demonstrate what a ministry leader needs to know to help a community get through the process.

to authorities. The rescue phase requires immediate response. It occurs in hours or days after the event.

In the **relief phase**, officials, disaster relief teams, non-profits, and volunteers arrive to provide the basic necessities of food, water, clothing, and shelter. Those who help during this phase also hope to provide spiritual or emotional support and make sure the people affected are safe from further harm. In this phase, the focus is on survival and stabilization. The relief phase involves short-term response. It takes days or weeks.

During the **recovery phase**, VOADs, government groups, non-profits, volunteers, and local officials help residents restore their lives and property. This includes restoring essential services, such as electricity, water, and communication systems; rebuilding infrastructure, homes, and public buildings; and supporting economic recovery for the community. This is also the time in which the long-term health, psychological, and social needs of the affected population are addressed. In this phase, the focus is on rebuilding and restoring. The recovery phase is a long-term response. It lasts for months or years.

Phases of Disaster Recovery

Rescue phase	Immediate response	Hours or days
Relief phase	Short-term response	Days or weeks
Recovery phase	Long-term response	Months or years

There is always frustration, misinformation, social media gossip, and conflict when a disaster occurs. Much of that is caused by the lack of understanding about these three phases. For example, in West, we set up what we called the "Long-Term Recovery Center." That was the place where everyone could go to find help and learn about available resources. Early on, the money that was donated for long-term recovery efforts had not yet been released to us, but people were donating items to the center to be distributed to those who had been affected by the explosion. When survivors came into the center to get help, they could receive those donated items. Since the name of the facility was "Long-Term Recovery Center," some of the people thought that was all they were going to receive, and those donated items were not even close to what they had lost. The donated items were intended to be short-term solutions to meet immediate needs while we waited for the long-term solutions to come later. Perhaps the center should have been called by another name until the long-term recovery funds were available, but none of us had ever been through an experience like that, and we had to learn as we went. It was years later when I was studying disaster recovery that I realized some of that confusion arose because we were not thinking about the phases and how they differ. It is easy to see how misunderstandings like that can happen when people are looking for phase three answers but all that is available at the time are phase two solutions.

Understanding the recovery process in three phases instead of one long journey helps everyone involved know what to expect, how to adapt, and how to be the most helpful in each phase. There are three groups for whom this information is essential: donors, volunteers, and ministry leaders.

Donors

Almost every time there is a disaster anywhere in the United States, we hear about funds being established so donors can send money to help the victims. In most cases, we soon hear about people getting upset about that money or questioning where it is going. That common confusion derives from not understanding the process and not recognizing the differences between the short-term relief phase and the long-term recovery phase.

I have been asked many times if it is better to give money to local churches and non-profits or to the big funds that are established through foundations and banks and advertised on TV. That debate comes up after almost every major event. We usually hear someone encourage donors to give to the church or the non-profit because they get the money to the people right away. Others argue that if you give your money to those organizations, it might not get used in the current disaster but set aside for the next one. Some will see a great deal of money coming into the large funds being managed by banks or foundations and ask why that money is not being immediately distributed. All these common reactions are based on a misunderstanding of the phases in the recovery process. When I am asked whether disaster donations should be made to churches and non-profits or the big funds, my answer is simple: "Give to both!" When you compare the two types of donations, you compare apples and oranges. They serve different functions, meet different needs, and are distributed at different times.

When you give to local churches and non-profits, you are supporting their efforts during the *short-term relief* phase. That money will be used to help people find shelter, buy food and clothing, get medical care, find transportation, etc. That money is distributed quickly and directly because it is not intended to help restore people's lives and enable them to rebuild and recover, it is just enough to keep them going. When you give to the large funds established at banks and foundations, you are supporting the hard work of *long-term recovery*. That money will not be distributed immediately because it involves a much more complicated distribution process. There must be time for all the fund-raising efforts to conclude so those managing the funds can know how much money there is to be used. There are also regulations on how 501(c)(3) foundations process funds, and the IRS has regulations on how recipients use and report those funds. Case workers are often hired and trained so they can evaluate the needs of each household, and the money can be distributed in ways that will not cause tax issues or other concerns for the recipients. People do receive help more quickly from money that is donated to local churches and non-profits, but they do not receive enough money at that time to meet major needs. They have to wait longer to get money from the foundations and banks, but those donations are larger and can be handled in ways that protect the recipients from taxation. Short-term relief helps the families have what they need so they can concentrate on figuring out their path for recovery and determining what their greatest needs are. Then, long-term funds are available to help them meet those needs and accomplish their recovery.

People who have been affected by the disaster do not even know what their needs are until they have had time to move through the short-term relief phase, evaluate their losses, work with their insurance, receive their medical bills, etc. Well-meaning donors might not understand that people in short-term relief are not ready for long-term funds. Not long after our explosion, I was contacted by a large church in my state. They said they wanted to take care of me and my family, and all I had to do was tell them how much I needed. I got a similar offer from a pastor friend who said he had a network of pastors who could raise whatever money my family and I needed to rebuild our home and get reestablished. Both of them were just waiting for me to let them know how much we needed.

The problem was they were asking for long-term information while I was still in short-term relief mode. We lost our home in the explosion, and we moved four times in the first six weeks, depending on the hospitality and generosity of others. I was eating donated food, driving a borrowed truck, living in other people's homes, and wearing other people's clothes. I was working from sunup until late into the night every day, helping as many people as I could. That went on for many months. I simply had no time to evaluate our own losses or begin planning to rebuild. By the end of the sixth week, my family and I were safe and comfortable in housing that had been set up for us by a friend, so I could put our recovery on hold to help keep everything going in the community. Because of all that, I did not have any answers for my would-be benefactors. I eventually let them know they did not need to wait on us any longer; we would be OK. The big church generously sent us some gift cards to help us get back on our feet, and my pastor friend found other ways to help us and the community. Once our disaster was behind us and I could think about all that had happened, I realized what the problem was: my donors were offering to help with long-term recovery issues, but I was still sorting out short-term relief problems.

When the explosion happened, we did not have a charitable foundation established in West, so as funds came in from all over the country, those funds were held at a couple of banks and at a well-established foundation in a neighboring town. That foundation held the funds until we could establish our own local foundation and get it approved as a 501(c)(3) charitable organization.

Even then, they were hesitant to release the funds because our newly formed "West, Texas Foundation" was inexperienced with handling money and needed to prove that we could manage it properly. While our board navigated through that process, some of us local leaders continued to work through churches and other charities to ensure that immediate and short-term needs were being met. A great deal of money and other resources were distributed during that short-term phase, but some of our opponents chose to direct the news media to focus on the money being held by the foundation who was helping us prepare for the long-term phase. They reported that the money was not being distributed, and they effectively ignored the millions of dollars in various short-term resources that were being distributed to meet immediate needs. When we moved into the long-term recovery phase, people had been able to properly assess their unmet needs and began receiving medical bills and construction costs, which is when the long-term funds being held at the neighboring foundation were released to West and distribution began.

Much of the donors' confusion and resentment would be alleviated if more people understood how the two major phases of recovery require different funds at different times. In the aftermath of Hurricane Helene in October of 2024, much was said about FEMA only giving affected families $750 after they lost everything in the terrible storm. The confusion was based on the common lack of understanding about the difference between short-term relief and long-term recovery. Those distributions of $750 were part of FEMA's Serious Needs Assistance, which is intended for immediate needs that are a part of short-term relief. [2] Accepting one of those immediate grants does not disqualify a

---

2.   More information about FEMA's Serious Needs Assistance is available at https://www.fema.gov/sites/default/files/documents/fema_ia-quick-reference_serious-needs.pdf

family from receiving additional funds later as part of their long-term recovery.

Volunteers

When disasters happen, volunteers show up. Many of those volunteers are people who live close to the affected area and feel a comradery with their neighbors in need. There are also many people who have been affected by a previous disaster and have learned the value of volunteerism, so they want to help others who are hurting like they once were. There is still another group of volunteers (perhaps the largest of the three) who are organized and trained for disaster response. Groups like these, including the On Mission Network, United Methodists Committee On Relief, Samaritan's Purse, Salvation Army, etc., have people who sacrificially go from one disaster to the next, responding to the needs of victims. In recent decades, it has become popular to denigrate what many refer to as "organized religion," but when your world falls apart, you will desperately hope that "organized religion" shows up, and you will be grateful when they do.

Those who volunteer to help people after disasters should understand the phases of the process so they can provide the most effective care. Usually, volunteers appear and serve during the short-term relief phase. They are there to help provide meals, clothing, shelter, water, boxes for packing up belongings, and a long list of other kinds of ministry that are intended to meet immediate needs.

When those volunteers arrive, they need to remember that people affected by the disaster are still in that short-term, foggy haze that characterizes the relief phase. They are scared, tired, hungry, and most likely irritable. Volunteers who understand the nature of the relief phase can better understand those emotions and bring calming reassurance into an otherwise chaotic experience. It is also helpful for volunteers to avoid expecting the people they serve to have a long-term plan or asking questions that cannot be answered until the long-term recovery phase begins.

Volunteers who understand the phases of recovery are also better equipped to pray for the people they are serving. They can pray about things that are appropriate for the phase in which the affected persons are working. During the relief phase, volunteers can pray for God's provision, protection, and comfort, for the details of everyday life, and for food, a place to sleep, necessary transportation, opportunities for communication with family, etc. As the affected persons transition into the recovery phase, there is less urgency and emotion. Pray for the long-range plans, the big bills that are piling up, the repair or construction of the homes, healing from injuries, etc.

Volunteers who understand the phases of recovery will see the importance of what they do to provide immediate assistance but will also continue to think about, pray for, and minister to their new friends throughout the long-term recovery phase. The news media is there only for the short-term relief phase, and then most people forget about those affected when they move into the very difficult, tiring, and arduous work of long-term recovery. Volunteers who recognize the need can continue to reach out and encourage the victims long after everyone else's attention has moved on to the new headlines of the day.

In Luke 10:25–37, Jesus told a parable that we usually refer to as "The Good Samaritan." Given the primary purpose of the story and the context in which Jesus told it, a better title would be "The Good Neighbor." In that well-known parable, the Samaritan sees a man on the side of the road who has been beaten and robbed and left for dead. The Samaritan chooses to help the man in need and does so in two phases. First, he meets the immediate needs—treating and bandaging the wounds and taking the man to an inn for shelter and medical care. When the Samaritan leaves the inn the next day, he gives the innkeeper some money and asks him to continue to care for the one who was hurting. The good neighbor even promises to return to pay whatever else is owed. He met the short-term relief needs of first aid, transportation, housing, and money for food. Then, he promised to return, thus assuring his care through the long-term recovery phase as well. That is a valuable volunteer and a good neighbor indeed.

Ministry Leaders

After a disaster, people tend to reorganize their priorities, and they are reminded of their need for God. Because of that, pastors and ministry leaders have greater opportunities to have an influence on the people in their community. Disasters do not just open doors to your community; they blow those doors off their hinges! September 16, 2001, is often said to have been the highest church attendance date in U.S. history. That was the Sunday after the terrorist attacks on September 11. In the wake of the national tragedy, churches across the country experienced a massive surge in attendance. Many people sought solace, comfort, and guidance in the aftermath of the attack. Disasters have a way of getting people's attention and turning them to the church for answers. Crisis is fuel for the Gospel.

It is essential that pastors and ministry leaders understand the significance of the different phases of recovery. How ministers lead and speak to those in their community should be informed by the phase in which they find themselves. Offering long-term solutions for short-term issues could make the minister appear disconnected or irrelevant. Continuing to address short-term problems after most people have moved on to searching for long-term solutions could make the minister appear shallow, short-sighted, or, worst of all, lacking the faith to move and lead others forward. What then should a pastor or ministry leader say and do in each phase? Base your teaching, preaching, social media presence, and personal conversations on specific themes that are appropriate for each phase.

During the chaotic, fast-paced, confusing, and fearful short-term relief phase, people need to hear about **God's providence**. You probably will not use that word often but let the glorious reality of God's presence and power guide your thinking, speaking, and behavior. Let His providence be your guiding light through the fog. The people with whom you minister after a devastating event need to be reassured of God's presence with them. They need to know that they are safe. Security will have immediately moved from a routine expectation to a desperate need. Address that by telling your people about God's love for them. Let them know that even though this event was terrible, and it seems too big to overcome, God is able to take care of them. We used our theme "God is bigger than all of this" for the first few months after the explosion. It brought us the faith and courage that we needed to keep going.

The leader's theme in the long-term recovery phase moves from providence to hope. As we transitioned into the long-term recovery phase, our theme became, "God is good, and West is blessed." During that phase, people get tired, and frustrated, and they begin to wonder if they will ever get back to "normal." As they work harder than ever, they can only see the work yet to be done. There is often an understandable temptation to give up. The people with whom you minister in times like that need hope. Reassure them that God saw all this coming and is able to see them through it. They need to be reminded that God has helped them thus far in their recovery and is currently blessing them, even if they cannot see it yet. The Psalmist sang of the power of hope in Psalm 33:20–22, "Our soul waits for the LORD; he is our help and our shield. For our heart is glad in him, because we trust in his holy name. Let your steadfast love, O LORD, be upon us, even as we hope in you."

The Rule of Ten

People in disaster recovery circles are familiar with what is often called "The Rule of Ten."[3] It is a general principle that can be helpful in determining the expected timing of the phases. Pastors and ministry leaders will find the Rule of Ten helpful in planning how to lead people and respond to their needs in appropriate ways. The rule begins with observing the time it takes to work through the initial rescue phase of a disaster. That involves the time necessary to rescue the injured, recover the remains of the deceased, locate the missing, and confirm that the danger has passed. Using that length of time as a base, one can estimate how long the short-term relief phase will last by multiplying by ten. For example, if the rescue phase takes three days, it can be estimated

---

3. I was first introduced to the Rule of Ten by a presentation to leaders in West during our recovery. That presentation was based on information found in the Congregational Disaster Preparedness Guidebook published by Lutheran Disaster Response of the Evangelical Lutheran Church in America.

that the relief stage will take approximately 30 days. One then multiplies the answer by ten to estimate how long the recovery phase might take. In our example, 30 days of relief would suggest 300 days of recovery.

RESCUE PHASE X10 → RELIEF PHASE X10 → RECOVERY PHASE

Our disaster in West was unique in that the event happened instantaneously. It was not like a hurricane or tornado that come with warnings and last until the storm weakens or moves on. Our explosion happened in a moment, and the devastation was immediate. However, our rescue phase took many days. It took about ten days for us to make sure everyone was accounted for and that the north side of town was safe enough for residents to return to their homes and begin the relief phase. That ten-day rescue phase translated roughly into 100 days (over three months) of short-term relief, as we tried to put things back together well enough to make our long-term plans. Multiplying the length of our relief phase by ten estimates our recovery time at 1,000 days or a little less than four years. That is pretty accurate for most of the households that were affected. As a community, it took us longer than that because we had major city infrastructure problems to solve, but the Rule of Ten was accurate for most of the families in West.

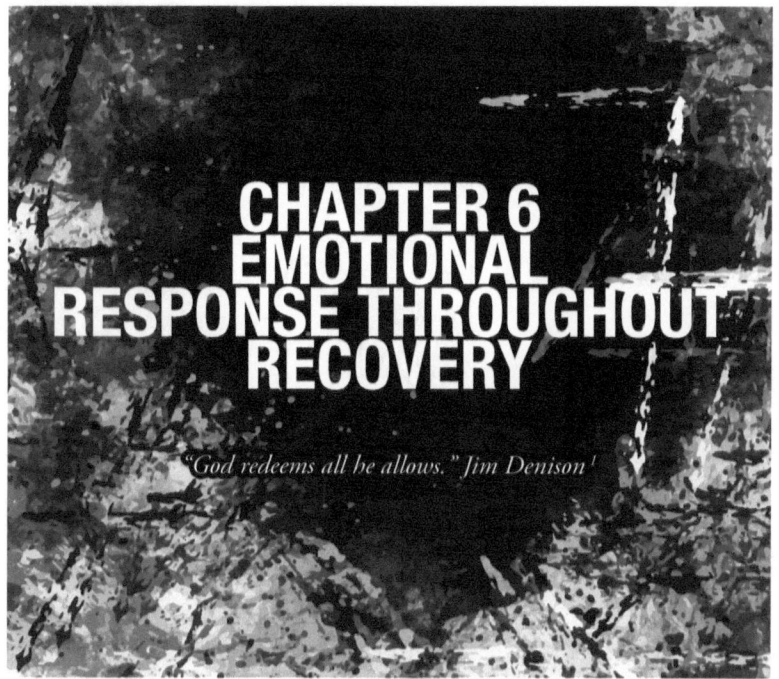

CHAPTER 6
EMOTIONAL
RESPONSE THROUGHOUT
RECOVERY

"God redeems all he allows." Jim Denison [1]

Every disaster is unique, and every community is unique. However, the emotional responses of most communities follow similar tracks throughout their recovery experiences. The graph below depicts those responses. An early version of the graph was included in a publication by the Substance Abuse and Mental Health Services Administration of the U.S. Department of Health and Human Services (HHS) and the Federal Emergency Management Agency (FEMA). [2]

1.   Jim Denison, PhD, "Does God Redeem All He Allows?", Daily Article, denisonforum.org, March 24, 2016, Denison Forum of Denison Ministries, https://www.denisonforum.org/daily-article/does-god-redeem-all-he-allows/. Also see J. Denison, *Wrestling With God: How Can I Love a God I'm Not Sure I Trust?*, (Tyndale House Publishers, 2008), Chapter 7.

2.   L. M. Zunnin & D. Meyers, "Phases of disasters," *Training Manual for Mental Health and Human Service Workers in Major Disasters*, 2nd ed., DHHS publication no. ADM 90–358.

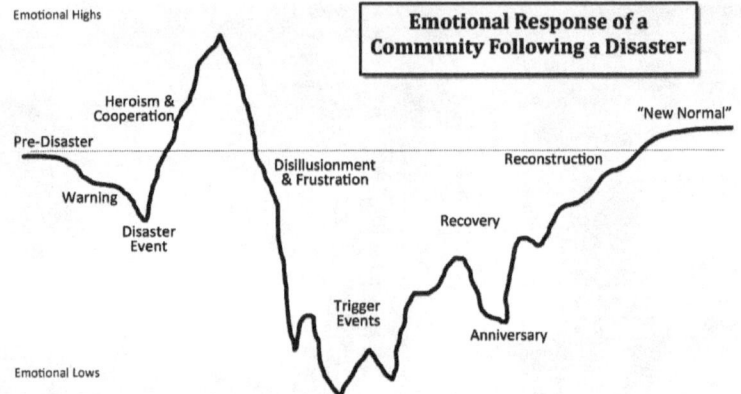

Adapted from publications by the Substance Abuse and Mental Health Services Administration (SAMHSA) of the U.S. Department of Health and Human Services and the Federal Emergency Management Agency (FEMA) of the U.S. Department of Homeland Security.

Overview

The graph reflects the emotional highs and lows that most communities experience as they endure a disaster and go through a recovery process. As expected, the emotional response of a community drops drastically when a disaster occurs, but then, there is a climb as the community rallies together. The fall that follows that short-lived climb, however, is usually steep and rapid. Over time, the community does the hard work necessary to climb back up, and there is a surprise ending.

Warning and Event

In natural disasters like hurricanes or tornadoes, there may be a warning that precedes the actual event. When that warning comes, the community involved responds with fear, anxiety, stress, and perhaps even panic. The graph shows those responses as it points downward into the "emotional lows." That downward trend ends at the disaster event.

The Quick Climb

Once the event is concluded, people feel relief. Even though the losses and pain are great, they can at least be comforted by the fact that the event is over. Those feelings of relief and relative security quickly lead to a climb in emotional response. The community rallies together as residents begin helping one another, encouraging each other, and cooperating in their efforts to clean up debris, evaluate their losses, establish safe living arrangements, and procure adequate medical attention, food, and water. Immediately after our explosion, the Red Cross came to West to help set up temporary housing. They were surprised to discover that no one requested their help. Everyone in West had friends or family who took them in during those first few days, and we all took care of each other.

Immediately after a shared disaster, neighbors who have not spoken to each other in years begin cooperating. People who have more resources begin helping those who suffered greater losses. Local people begin working hard and working together, while volunteers from neighboring communities start showing up to help. This is the period in which volunteerism is praised, and local heroes are honored. It is sometimes referred to as the "Honeymoon Stage,"[3] but the phrase seems out of place in the context of disaster recovery, so I choose not to use it. There is a short-lived optimism and positive outlook on the future. Communities often celebrate their strength and resilience by inserting the name of their town in common phrases like "Boston Strong." That climb in the emotional response graph continues upward beyond where they were in their "normal" lives before the event. For a little while,

3. For example, C. Bowenkamp, "Coordination of mental health and community agencies in disaster response," *International Journal of Emergency Mental Health*, (2000): 159–165.

there is almost a euphoria, full of pride and hope, but it does not last long. The fall from that high is dramatic.

The Long, Hard Fall

Soon after the emotional highs of pride, heroism, cooperation, and newly discovered strength come the harsh realities of pain, loss, grief, confusion, and helpless frustration. The drastic emotional fall is well depicted in the graph, as the line turns sharply downward and descends quickly into the lowest points of the recovery experience. During this rapid descent, stories of heroism become old news, the initial volunteers begin their retreat, funerals are held, compassionate reports in the news are replaced by negative stories, fatigue sets in, anger begins to brew, rumors and accusations run rampant, and hope is rare. It is during this time that most people learn that insurance companies are businesses, not friends or neighbors. Government agencies are massive bundles of red tape, and working with them requires time and patience, which most people do not have when recovering from a disaster. The people who were affected by the disaster begin to feel disillusioned, whoever was supposed to protect them did not. Whoever was supposed to help them wound up making things more difficult, and whoever was supposed to bring a conclusion to the recovery did not do so quickly or efficiently. They feel forgotten, ignored, neglected, or even belittled. Emotionally speaking, this is the worst time of the recovery process.

Trigger Events

If there is any good news about the deep decline just described, it is that there is a bottom to that pit. The fall into emotional lows does not continue forever. Eventually, the lowest part of the recovery process will occur, and the emotional response of the people involved will level out for a bit. As the community tries to pull itself out of the pit and find ways to make progress, there will inevitably be some events that trigger emotional setbacks. Someone who was injured in the event might die, and that funeral will bring back emotions from earlier funerals. The news media might present a report that shows the community in a negative light.[4] A beloved building or well-known landmark may have to be demolished. These and any number of similar events can trigger a decline back into the lower emotional responses.

In West, the ATF, FBI, and some state agencies planned a joint press conference in which they were going to announce the cause of the fire that led to the explosion. There was much anticipation leading up to the meeting because understanding what happened would bring some sense of closure and enable us to move forward more effectively. The official announcement, however, included three possible reasons for the fire with a declaration that we may never know for certain what happened.[5] That triggered a sharp emotional setback for many of us. Other triggering events included the demolition of our homes and schools, the end of the school year with no place to celebrate the usual rites of passage, and discussions about pending lawsuits.

The Slow Ascent

From the depths of disillusionment and despair, survivors begin to climb. Their journey will eventually take them to new

---

4.   See the later discussion in Chapter 9 about news media.
5.   A long time later, government officials announced that two of the possible causes for the initial fire had been ruled out, leaving arson as the only remaining option.

heights, but the journey to get there is difficult, tiring, and lengthy. Some of my church family and I took a mission trip to Honduras several years ago. We wanted to visit a village that was set on the side of a mountain. To get to it, we had to drive to the mountaintop and walk down the side of the mountain to the village. That part was a little challenging for me, but it went well. We got to the village and had a wonderful time with the people there. The problem came when it was time to leave the village and take the trek back up to the top of the mountain where our vehicles were. I was not used to that kind of exercise. I had to stop climbing every few feet to sit for a minute and catch my breath. I was the last to arrive, but I did finally make it to the top. The missionary told me I looked like a "dead bird." That climb was one of the most physically challenging journeys of my life. Without question, the most challenging *emotional* climb of my life was recovering from our disaster. The two journeys were very different but shared some common elements. Both experiences required more of me than I would have expected. They both required some rest stops along the way, and they both required determination. No matter how difficult the climb was, I was determined to finish the trip.

The road to recovery includes that long, hard climb that takes up over half of the graph. Although the line moves upward, it is not a straight line. Emotional highs and lows are inherent in recovery. There will be days when survivors feel like they have helped each other make progress, and there will be days when obstacles or delays bring disappointment or discouragement. Over time, the good days begin to outnumber the bad ones, and eventually, there are enough good days to make that line climb more steadily.

As you and your community climb, celebrate everything you can. Rejoice over every advance and victory. Our motto during the long-term recovery phase was "God is good, and West is blessed." It served as a reminder that even though the climb was tough, God was at work, and we were finally able to see some of the results of that work. The more we celebrated God's goodness, the more we were able to find it and the more we could accomplish together.

Anniversary

The first anniversary after the event is the most difficult. The pain is still fresh; grief is still a part of the daily struggle for many. In most disasters, when the date of the event arrives the following year, it occurs while the emotional response is still low, so it serves as a hard reminder of all that has happened and how the survivors still have a long way to go in their recovery. Later anniversaries get easier and can even become positive experiences when seen as mile markers along the journey. They serve to remind survivors of how far they have come. This first anniversary, however, will most likely bring a sharp decline in emotional response. It is a difficult one to get through.

Reconstruction

When reconstruction finally begins, and there is enough progress being made that it is visibly evident in the community, the emotional response climbs upward at a more consistent and steadier pace. Seeing new buildings being built, infrastructure being repaired, wounds healing, kids going back to school in their own neighborhoods, and residents returning to new homes can bring great relief and even joy to those who have been through so much turmoil in the recent past. The realization that recovery is nearing its end, and the community has made real progress can invigorate and energize survivors to finish strong.

"New Normal"

"New normal" is a phrase that gets used often in disaster recovery conversations. It refers to the re-established, settled lifestyle that is achieved toward the end of the recovery process. Necessary changes and adjustments have been made, and the survivors are learning to be at home in their new surroundings. It is here that the graph depicts a surprising ending. Often, the overall emotional response of the community is higher in its "new normal" than it was before the whole ordeal began. Many times, we hear mayors, governors, or other leaders speak immediately following a disaster. Those early speeches are intended to give hope to the people affected. Usually, the leader will say something like, "We will come back. We will rebuild. We will be stronger than ever." It turns out that, whether they actually believe that or not, they are usually speaking the truth. In most cases, communities that work together to help one another through recovery do come out stronger on the other side. The "new normal" on the chart is a little higher than the pre-disaster normal was.

Leading Through the Chart

It is essential for pastors and ministry leaders to understand the chart as they lead people through recovery, so they can understand what is happening and why people are behaving the way they are. Leaders also need to be prepared for the next expected fall or climb in emotional response. By understanding it and anticipating it, leaders can be better equipped to guide their people through it.

When the disaster event is occurring, there is little the leader can do but ride it out. Once the event is over and recovery has been initiated, the leader can begin their work. After the immediate responses described in Chapter 2, point your people to every source of hope you can find. Celebrate the cooperation and the volunteerism that is taking place. Honor the first responders and other heroes in your story. Survivors will be headed in that direction anyway, and you want to encourage it as a means of helping them climb out of their initial despair.

After the "quick climb" reaches its peak and you sense the beginning of the "long, hard fall," hold on. You're about to enter deep waters—take a deep breath, and be ready to swim against the current. You will work harder than ever before. You will be exhausted, and your list of things to do will seem never ending. It will be particularly frustrating if you suffered personal losses and have to manage your own recovery while helping others manage theirs. No matter how hard you work or how much you give, be ready for the negative reactions of the people around you. Even though it will be difficult, get as much rest as you can, eat nutritious food regularly, and lead your people with optimism and hope. They may not realize how much they appreciate it at first, but it is essential for you to care for them in these ways, as they face the most difficult days of their lives.

At each trigger event, be present with the survivors. If explanations are helpful, share them, but most likely the people you serve will benefit more from your presence during those times than from any wise words you might have to offer. Walk through this experience with your people. Carry the burdens, acknowledge the grief, and share the journey. When Tauren Wells sings about the "Hills and Valleys" of life, he testifies that just as we are not alone when things are going well:

When I'm walking through the valley
I know I am not alone.[6]

Even though you must see the people you love suffer, remember that the fall to the depths of despair is part of the process, and you will not have to endure it alone. Remind yourself as you remind the people around you that God is walking through the valley with you and will see you through. When Israel was at their lowest, God reminded them through the prophet, "When you pass through the waters, I will be with you; and through the rivers, they shall not overwhelm you; when you walk through fire you shall not be burned, and the flame shall not consume you" (Isaiah 43:2).

As the community begins its slow ascent into brighter days, celebrate everything you can find to celebrate. Every little step forward is worth acknowledging and expressing gratitude. You can help the people climb higher and faster with consistent words of encouragement and hope. Let them hear hope from you and see dedicated service from you. Speak often with words of comfort, but also work hard to carry more than your share of the load. Lead by example and let them see in you that the climb is worth the effort.

---

6.   Chuck Butler, Jonathan Smith, and Tauren Wells, "Hills and Valleys," ©Be Essential Songs, Cashagamble Jet Music, Crucial Music Entertainment, Hipgnosis Songs Essential, Jord A Lil Music, So Essential Tunes, administered by Provident Label Group LLC, a division of Sony Music Entertainment, 2017.

When that first anniversary comes, face it head on. Have a plan for a gathering of some kind. Point out what your people probably cannot see on their own yet—they are making progress. Honor the heroes again, and respectfully remember those who did not survive. This first anniversary will set the stage for the other anniversaries to come. Make it memorable, positive, and hopeful. One idea that I have seen work well is to speak about a new day dawning on the community. Speak about the sun rising on a new era for your community. Treat that day as the mark of a new beginning.

Through the rest of the recovery, keep encouraging your people to focus on the future. Speak often about next steps, progress, and dedication to success. If you have the opportunity for formal preaching or teaching, talk about the continued need for service and love, the power of faith and hope, the need for unity and cooperation, and the truth of God's providence and presence throughout the recovery process.[7]

As you near the completion of recovery, help your people see how far they have come and all they have accomplished. As noted earlier, we often refer to the conclusion of recovery as a "new normal." That phrase is accurate in many ways because life has certainly changed by the time you arrive at the end of recovery. Nonetheless, there are a few reasons to be careful with that saying.

First, it must be used at the right time. Be careful not to define the recovery process itself as the "new normal." You do not want people to think they have to settle for life in recovery from now on. During the COVID pandemic, I cringed each time I heard a reporter refer to distancing, masks, and shutdowns as our "new normal." That was not normal, and we were never intended to

---

7. There are some other preaching/teaching ideas included in the appendix.

settle for that lifestyle long term. It was a necessary short-term response to tragedy. We had to go through a specific kind of recovery, but our goal was the establishment of a safe and healthy "new normal" that could only come on the other side of recovery.

Another reason we want to be careful when using the phrase is that we do not want to send the message that we are forgetting our past, disrespecting the memory of those we lost, or belittling our old way of life. As long as those misunderstandings are intentionally avoided, celebrating the "new normal" at the right time can be beneficial and joyous.

When the process is complete and your community has an overall higher emotional response than it did prior to the disaster, build on that. Keep making progress, starting new things, and finding reasons to celebrate. You will be able to lead your people to do more than you would have had they never been through a tragedy.

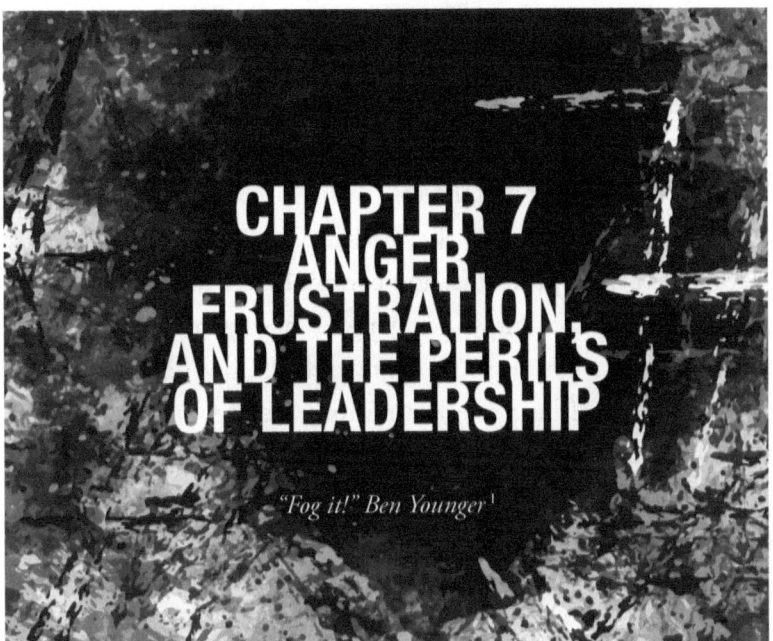

CHAPTER 7
ANGER FRUSTRATION, AND THE PERILS OF LEADERSHIP

"Fog it!" Ben Younger[1]

As demonstrated in the previous chapter, part of the recovery process includes disillusionment. That leads to stress, frustration, and anger. Some of those reactions are often directed toward the people who have stepped up to help lead the community through the crisis. As people try to make sense of the devastation around them and the chaos that engulfs them, they need someone to blame. If they feel like someone is at fault, there can be some explanation to the confusion or at least some semblance of justice. Expectedly, that leads to finger pointing, false assumptions, and accusing the very leaders who are trying to help because it is those leaders who are in the people's line of vision. People know they can't get mad at a storm, a fire, or a bunch of water, but the first people they see taking some responsibility become easy targets for their angry outbursts.

---

1. Ben Younger was a Methodist minister, educator, philanthropist, community builder, and a personal friend.

Most of the first half of our recovery was awful for me. I refer to it as my "second disaster." I have never worked so hard and been under such attack. I started early in the morning and went until late at night, working to assess needs, finding resources for assistance, helping to connect volunteers with victims, communicating with the community and the media, participating in meetings, planning, solving problems, and continuing all my regular duties as a full-time pastor, all while trying to manage my own personal recovery. Each night, I would come to the mobile home where we were staying and hear another misinformed report on the local news or find another unfair attack on social media. My blood pressure was high, I could not sleep without medication, and my stress was off the charts.

The turning point of my recovery occurred when I made a new friend. Ben Younger was at a school board meeting. He sat off to the side and did not speak much, but he was clearly interested in the conversation about how the school district was going to move forward. After the meeting, we walked out of the building together. He introduced himself and engaged me in a conversation as we made our way to my truck. Almost immediately I sensed I was in the presence of a wise caregiver. In the days that followed, that first impression was confirmed.

Fog It

Ben had been through difficult times before, and he had helped many others get through difficult times as well. When I needed to talk, Ben was there. Sometimes he even arrived unannounced to encourage me or give me a break. It was during one of those healing conversations that I told him about my exhaustion and the pain I felt from all the verbal assaults I had to endure. I noticed a grin beginning to form behind his bushy beard. It was his signature grin that meant, "I can't wait to see your reaction to the advice I'm about to give you." As I prepared myself for the profound wisdom that was certainly on its way, I was surprised when he only said two words: "Fog it!"

His response snapped me out of my self-pity and ignited my curiosity. I asked what he meant, and his explanation gave me a new, life-changing perspective. "If you are stiff and rigid like a pane of glass, you will shatter when people throw rocks at you. But if you are like fog, the rocks people throw just go right on through and fall to the ground without affecting you. Fog it!"

Several times over the next few weeks, I would get upset or defensive, and he would remind me, "Fog it!" Soon, I was able to remind myself. Ben and I became great friends. When he passed on, I was honored to conduct his funeral. Years later, when people say or do hurtful things, I think of Ben, take a deep breath, and fog it.

In a world full of glass, where people are constantly getting shattered and trying to shatter those around them, fog it! That does not mean that we no longer take a stand for truth and justice. It simply means that when we're attacked on a personal level, we have some say in how much damage that attack causes. In most cases, we can decide to let a personal attack sail on by without allowing it to break us into pieces. When someone is intentionally hurtful, unfair, or rude, we get to decide how much their words will impact us. If the other person's goal is to hurt me and I let myself break into pieces, they have been successful, so they win. If, on the other hand, I choose not to let their words affect me, they fail, and I win! I have found great freedom and tremendous strength in that lesson from Ben. There are times when we need to just fog it!

This life lesson is particularly valuable during recovery. The folks you serve will not always appreciate your sacrifice. They will not understand all the complicated issues that are involved in solving the problems facing your community. During the inevitable disillusionment period of recovery, they will most likely let their frustrations out at those who are in their line of sight. They see the leaders, so those leaders are the only people with whom the hurting victims can express their anger. Expect it, understand its origin, and find someone you can trust to help you process it. Work through it, but do not ever let it keep you from serving. God put you in that position of leadership, knowing that the disaster was on its way. You were chosen to serve those people in that place "for such a time as this" (Esther 4:14).

The cost of leadership is always great. Sometimes it costs physical excursion. Sometimes it requires emotional pain and distress. Other times leadership demands sacrificing popularity to do what is best for the people being served. During disaster recovery, part of the cost of leadership includes being a target. Lead anyway. There is a reason that when God called Joshua to lead the people into the Promised Land, He reminded Joshua to, "Be strong and courageous. Do not be afraid; do not be discouraged, for the LORD your God will be with you wherever you go" (Joshua 1:9 NIV). A common phrase among believers today bears repeating: "If God brought you to it, God will bring you through it." Remember also the great quote from the Prince of Preachers, Charles H. Spurgeon: "You may think that the Lord hath passed you by, but he hath not: he that counteth the stars, and calleth them all by name, hath no limit to his understanding, and no measure to his knowledge; he bindeth up the broken in heart, and healeth their wounds; and he knows your case and state as much and as perfectly as if you were the only creature he had ever made, or the only saint he had ever loved."[2] Depend on the Almighty One, and lead on!

Filter It

Without question, Ben's advice was one of the greatest leadership lessons I ever learned. The freedom and the peace it brought me enabled me to endure the hard days and make it through. In implementing Ben's wisdom, however, I have also learned that leaders should avoid too quickly dismissing the complaints and concerns of those who speak up. Even in the anger of harsh words and the venom of personal attacks, there may be something worth hearing. How then does the leader choose whether to "fog it" or to hear it? The leader must learn to filter it.

Ask two questions. First, do not settle for anything less than an honest answer to the hard question, "Is the person **right**?" When we feel like we are under attack, our defenses go up, and we reject anything that seems like it might cause pain. When we are in that mode, however, we might miss out on a valuable opportunity for personal growth. Maybe there is some validity to the observations that are being expressed by the other person. Perhaps they can help us see something about ourselves or our organization that we might have missed without the benefit of their perspective. However it is also quite possible that what they are saying is not right. We cannot automatically assume

2.   Charles H. Spurgeon, *Metropolitan Tabernacle Pulpit, Vol. 10*, (London: Passmore & Alabaster, 1885). Sermon preached on November 6, 1864.

that because they are upset, they are correct. Anger is not always righteous anger. Often, people say and do things in anger that are not accurate, fair, or true. We need to wrestle with the question and be willing to determine the answer to the best of our ability: "Is the person right?"

The second question should be considered independently of the first. Setting aside your evaluation of the validity of the words, consider the manner in which the words were spoken or written. Ask, "Is the person being **reasonable**?" Regardless of how you answered the first question, you now must look at how they are treating you and whether or not their behavior is reasonable. If they are remaining calm, staying focused, and being fair in their choice of words, your response should be different than it would be if they were being hurtful, unfair, or overly dramatic.

Is the person right? Is the person being reasonable? The key to a rational response is identifying how the answers to those two questions work together. The two questions help us separate and process very different issues. Once we have adequately settled those issues, we can see how they relate to one another, and we can determine our response.

1. If the person **is right** and **is being reasonable**, give that person your full attention. You may set up a time to discuss their concerns later so you can adequately consider them, but you should let the person know they are being heard.

2. If the person **is right** but **is not being reasonable** about it, you are faced with a personal challenge. You should seriously weigh the content of the message without allowing the person to hurt your feelings or control you with his misbehavior. King Solomon taught us, "A soft answer turns away wrath, but a harsh word stirs up anger" (Proverbs 15:1). Listen to the ideas being expressed, but do

not validate the unreasonable words and actions.

3. If the person is **not right** but **is being reasonable**, listen respectfully and respond patiently in hope that you can help clarify their misunderstanding.

4. If the person is **not right** and is **not being reasonable**, protect yourself, and more importantly, protect your church or organization. You cannot do that by being bullied. Nor can you do that by giving in to the temptation to join in their misbehavior. You want to de-escalate the situation and walk away from it. You have to fog it!

True leaders do not serve for their own glory. Leaders do what they do because of love and a sense of calling. Love your community enough to lead it, even when it is difficult. Love and lead the people who are depending on you, even when they do not understand it or appreciate it. In the end, it will be worth every sacrifice, every tear, every hurt feeling. When the rocks come flying, don't be surprised; just filter it and fog it.

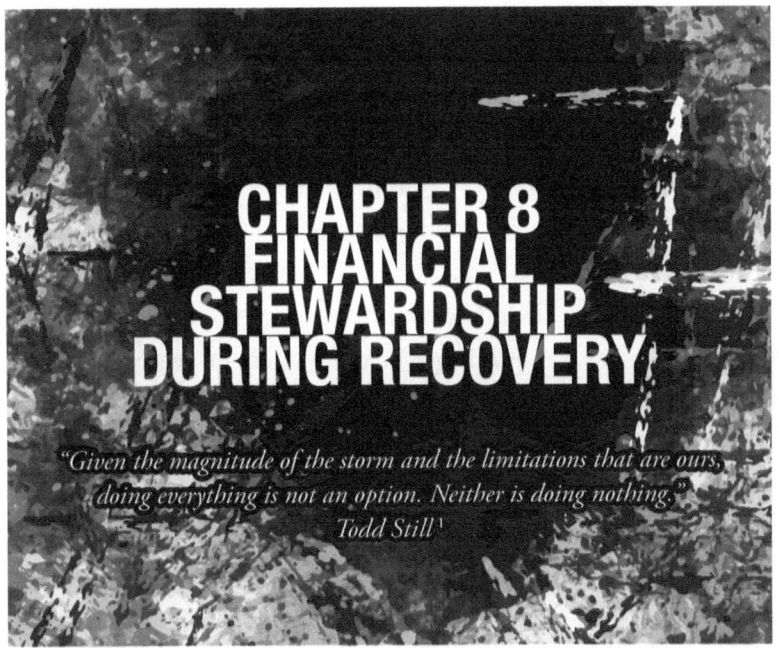

CHAPTER 8
FINANCIAL STEWARDSHIP DURING RECOVERY

"Given the magnitude of the storm and the limitations that are ours, doing everything is not an option. Neither is doing nothing."
Todd Still[1]

My father died when I was young, leaving my mother to finish raising four children on her own. She provided for our family and held us together admirably. We always had what we needed, but we did not have many luxuries. As a result, we did not have many conversations about personal finances, money management, investments, insurance, or mortgages. When those are not a part of family life, the topics rarely come up at the dinner table. When I grew up, I married a public school teacher and became a small-town pastor. In other words, we still did not have much money. For me, finances were like so many other things in life—we do not learn the important stuff until we have to. After the explosion, I had much to learn.

1. Todd Still, Dean of George W. Truett Seminary at Baylor University. This quote is from a statement Dr. Still made after the devastating and prolonged impact of Hurricane Harvey along the Texas coast in August of 2017.

Personal Finances

The West, Texas Foundation was responsible for distributing the donated funds during the long-term recovery phase. When I joined the board of that foundation, my first action was to disqualify myself from receiving any of the funds for which we would be responsible. I also serve as the treasurer of our local ministerial alliance, which distributed donated funds during the short-term relief phase. I disqualified myself from receiving any of those funds as well. Since my family and I could not receive donations like most of the other affected families, it was difficult for us to manage our finances and plan for our recovery. As described earlier, we missed out on a couple of opportunities for a great deal of financial assistance because it took us so long to get to the point where we could make the big decisions about our recovery. Because I was so busy, we lived in short-term relief mode longer than our potential donors expected. They were offering long-term solutions before we could determine how much we really needed.

A nameless gossip has tried a couple of times to start a rumor around town that I somehow benefited financially from the explosion. The truth is we wound up losing a great deal of money in the disaster, but all we lost was money and material things. Many people lost much more than that. We did not lose family members or loved ones. Therefore, we see our losses as minimal.

During our recovery, we did receive some generous personal donations. Our friends and family took care of us in countless ways. Some of the people who provided our demolition and construction donated their equipment, materials, and services or gave us discounts. Our friends provided us with a place to live while we got everything sorted out, and we even had a few strangers who had heard about us send money or gift cards. When our recovery was complete, we had lost some money, but because of the generosity of others and our own savings through the years, we made it just fine. We will always be grateful to those who helped us along the way.

Some of the people in West had insurance with companies who came into town, saw the devastation, and immediately started writing checks. We were not that fortunate. Our insurance adjuster spent most of a week recording every damaged rafter, counting each piece of wood, and calculating the cost of every nail that it would take to repair our house. We were also not able to replace all our belongings that were damaged or lost because we could only claim those for which we had receipts. Even then, each item we claimed was substantially reduced in value because of depreciation. The amount they finally paid us was not anywhere close to our actual losses.

I learned three lessons about insurance that are worth passing along to others who must undergo recovery from a massive loss. First, regardless of what you see in their television commercials, insurance companies are not there to be your friend or neighbor. Like all businesses, they exist to make money. That is not a bad thing. There is nothing wrong with offering a product or service and making a profit from it. As consumers, we just need to be aware that insurance companies exist to do business. They sell policies for as much as they can charge, and they pay out on those policies for as little as possible. As long as you understand the purpose and goals of the insurance companies, you can manage your expectations and work with them effectively.

Second, when buying insurance, you need to consider worst case scenarios and talk with your agent about what your policies actually provide in those events. Ask questions. Find out if your policy is intended to help make you whole or if it is intended to pay for each specific two-by-four and floor tile that will first be depreciated.

Third, when necessary, it is possible to call on independent adjusters. I had never heard of that until it was too late for me. I wish I had called in an independent adjuster and included a lawyer in our conversations with the insurance company. We settled too early and for far too little because I was already overwhelmed with the work that had to be done and the stress of trying to manage our recovery while helping others. Now, I wish I had spent the money and taken the time to call in other experts to help me negotiate with our insurance company.

As we worked on our own finances and I helped others sort out theirs, I learned another personal finance lesson worth passing along. It is a good idea to go to the bank early in your recovery and open a new account that is separate from your other accounts. All the donations, insurance money, FEMA funds, and other recovery-related income goes into that new account. Then, you can pay for your recovery out of that account. By doing that, you make it easier to ensure that you have used all the money you received during the recovery period in the way it was intended. Keeping track of your recovery in that one account also helps with taxes later when you have to report how much you gained or lost through the process.

Receiving Donations

Some of the financial lessons we learned relate to how churches and organizations accept donated funds. The first lesson and the one that must be stressed the most vigorously is that every community should have a foundation that is recognized by the IRS as a 501(c)(3) organization. Cities and big towns have plenty of those organizations, but small towns and unincorporated communities need to have at least one such foundation as well. Even if that foundation does nothing other than the required annual meeting to approve officers and budget, it is necessary that every community have one. When a disaster strikes, people want to help. Many of those potential donors will only give to 501(c)(3) organizations. In West, we never thought about it until after the explosion made it necessary. Most people assumed our ministerial alliance was a 501(c)(3), but at the time, it was not. We were just a group of cooperating churches and ministers who pooled our money to help people in need. Some of the other organizations in town had the 501(c)(3) designation but were not organized in a way that would allow them to receive and distribute funds after a disaster. A group of committed, caring community servants came together in our time of need to begin forming a new organization that would eventually file for 501(c)(3) and become the West, Texas Foundation. In its infancy, the group called themselves the Long-Term Recovery Board. Before they were an official non-profit, they recognized the need for a couple more people to help them get up and running. The mayor called me and asked me to consider being a part of that effort. As a result, I learned that if God calls you to do something, you have to do it, but if the mayor calls you, hang up immediately! Although the work was difficult and I jest about the mayor's call, I am proud to have been a part of it.

We had to organize the Foundation and get the IRS to recognize us as a non-profit, which can take a long time. In the meantime, we had to depend on the foundation in a neighboring community to hold the money until we could get established and demonstrate our readiness to distribute it appropriately. That delayed our distribution and recovery. If we had a 501(c)(3) established before we needed one, we could have avoided a lot of heartache and hassle when the need for it arose.

Foundations or non-profits are necessary in every community because they are the best organizations to receive money during disasters. People who want to help the victims generally trust 501(c)(3) organizations to handle their donations. Those donors can also receive tax deductions when they give to non-profits because it is considered a charitable donation. Additionally, many big foundations are willing to donate for disaster relief but can only give money to other 501(c)(3) organizations.

Since most foundations have policies that restrict their donations to other 501(c)(3) organizations, we had some problems when foundations wanted to make donations to my church. Contrary to popular expectations and understandings, churches are not necessarily 501(c)(3) organizations. Churches that meet the requirements of section 501(c)(3) of the Internal Revenue Code are automatically considered tax exempt and are not required to obtain recognition of exempt status from the IRS.[2] Since churches are automatically exempt, many do not go through the work of applying for and obtaining the 501(c)(3) status. That is particularly true for smaller, rural churches. I received numerous calls from well-intentioned foundations who told me their board wanted to send donations to the church, but they could not find us on the IRS list of approved 501(c)(3) organizations. I told them we were

---

2. For more information, see Internal Revenue Service Publication 1858 (Rev. 8-2015), Tax Guide for Churches and Religious Organizations.

automatically approved for tax exempt status but did not have the formal recognition of a 501(c)(3). That almost always disqualified us from receiving funds from foundations. Their policies would not allow them to give money to groups that did not appear in the IRS database. Churches and ministry organizations should give serious consideration to obtaining that IRS recognition, even though it is not required for normal business interactions and receipts.

Distributing Funds

Even more complicated than receiving funds after a disaster is the distribution of those funds. I met with my deacons soon after the explosion to formulate a plan for our church. We knew that money would be coming in, and we needed to help get it to the people who needed it as quickly and efficiently as possible. We set a specific amount of money that could be immediately distributed to each family with a simple application. If a family asked for more than that base amount, we had a committee of three people who were authorized to review the case and approve or deny the request. Those three people were appointed by the deacons and did not suffer property damage that would cause them to need any of the funds they were responsible for distributing. Once again, my associate pastor and partner in the ministry, Phil Immicke, did an amazing job coordinating our efforts. That arrangement worked well, as we were able to distribute a great deal of money during the short-term relief phase of the recovery.

The Long-Term Recovery Board, which eventually became the West, TX Foundation, formulated and implemented a plan for the distribution of funds that were intended for the long-term recovery phase. As a member of that board, I wanted to just start handing out money to anyone who needed it, but we could not do that. State regulations on boards, federal regulations on FEMA funds, IRS regulations on disbursement of disaster funds, and other regulations on nonprofit organizations made it impossible to handle this process quickly or simply. Since the IRS considered the donated money to be "charitable," we had to be able to show that the recipients needed that charity. For that reason, we had to use a process that proved need. Had we failed to do that, the recipients could have been required to pay taxes on the money they received, and in the worst-case scenario, the board members could have even faced legal liability.

We had received approximately 3.6 million dollars, but the estimated losses for local families were closer to 30 million. We had to distribute the money fairly, confidentially, and legally, and we had to do it in a way that would make it stretch as far as possible because we did not have enough to cover all the losses. Our process began with case workers. If someone was affected by the disaster, a case worker would lead them through the process of finding all the help available. They would deal with insurance companies first, then FEMA, then any other resources that were available. Once they had been able to get all the help they could find, the case workers would present their case to our Unmet Needs Committee. That committee was made up of over a dozen community members. In each case, the committee then recommended to our board how much of the limited funds we should consider distributing to the household's remaining needs. We were careful to protect the anonymity of the people who requested help. When each case came to the board, no names were attached to the case so committee members and board members could be objective and fair. Once distributions began, those were recorded appropriately, but the information remained private so no one in town knew their neighbor's personal business. That process was not simple, but it was effective and became a good model for other communities who experienced disasters after us.

One of the guiding principles in distribution of funds following a disaster is "Donor Intent." Pastors and ministry leaders are familiar with that concept if not the term itself. It simply means that when someone donates to your organization, it is important for you to determine to the best of your ability what their intent for that money was. Funds should always be applied according to the intent of the donor. If there is a need that is different than the purpose the donor had in mind when making the donation, the ministry leader should contact the donor to obtain permission to use it in a different way. Unless the donor agrees to change the intent of the gift, it must be applied as originally expected. Honoring donor intent when distributing funds is ethical, expedient, and wise. Leaders can avoid all kinds of problems and increase potential for future giving by being careful to practice this principle.

One of the other financial lessons we learned in our recovery is the multiplied value of providing demolitions. In most cases, insurance companies make a single payment to a household that has survived a disaster. That household can then use the insurance money for their recovery. If they have to demolish their damaged house, they can use the insurance money to pay for that demolition but that means they have less to use on rebuilding. Often, demolitions are not figured into insurance claims, so families wind up using money for demolition and not having as much as they expected for their rebuild. One of the great ways a church or ministry organization can use donated funds is to organize and provide demolitions. That not only saves families the cost of the demolition, but it also helps them keep their insurance money for rebuilding. Due to some generous donations to the church and a large construction company who loaned us the equipment, our volunteers were able to lead the effort to provide sixty-three families with demolitions. The Texas Baptist Men worked alongside one of our deacons who had some experience in that field. Eventually, they were able to hand off the work to the Long Term Recovery Center. Using money donated by students and faculty at Baylor University, the Long Term Recovery Center picked up where our volunteers left off and handled another thirty or so demolitions. In the end, every family in West who requested a demolition got one at no cost.

My family was one of those who benefitted from that unique ministry. I will always remember how difficult it was to say goodbye to our house. We loved that house, and even though it was badly damaged and could never have been repaired, it broke my heart to see it come down. It held so many memories and so much of our story. I was standing in the front yard, watching as my deacon Rusty got everything ready. When it was time to begin, Rusty stepped out of the excavator and came over to me. He put his hand on my shoulder, and in that life-changing moment, my deacon became my pastor. He talked with me and prayed for us. He took time to make sure I was emotionally ready for him to begin. As I unsuccessfully fought back the tears, I assured him I was ready. He got back on the equipment and began tearing down my house. Before he finished, my daughter, Ashley, came home and sat on the mailbox to watch him finish the job. As I saw her watching our house being torn apart, I hurt for her as much as I did for myself. As painful as it was to watch our home turned to rubble, it also brought us some hope. That day marked the end of our beloved home but the beginning of our recovery. Ecclesiastes reminds us there is "a time to break down, and a time to build up" (Ecclesiastes 3:3b). There had to be a demolition before there could ever be a new house. Like so many others in my community, my family would not have been able to accomplish all we did in our recovery if we had to use our inadequate insurance money for that demolition.

Advising Survivors

As a pastor or ministry leader, you may find yourself in the position to advise survivors on handling their finances during recovery. You do not want to seek out or orchestrate these opportunities, but they will most likely arise naturally. If you are able to assist others in recovery by giving them financial advice, here are three suggestions to remember.

First, during recovery, people are just trying to get through each day and make it to the next day. They are not thinking about keeping up with paperwork or filing documents. Encourage them to keep good financial records. Many survivors will not think about that on their own, but a simple reminder can make a big difference. Survivors who keep up with all the documentation about their receipts and expenditures are better equipped to file proper tax reports later. Having good records also helps them have a more realistic view of what they can afford to spend during recovery. If questions arise later about how donations were used, documentation can bring clarity and can help avoid potential conflicts.

Second, if you are working with survivors who are asking for help from FEMA, tell them not to give up too quickly. Often, FEMA will reject initial requests but will respond favorably to appeals. Perhaps that is their way of weeding out the people with the most valid needs. Tell your folks to just keep asking until their claim is approved or clearly and finally rejected.

The third suggestion is the most complicated, but it might be the most valuable. If a person loses their home or has severe damage to it, the mortgage company will see the home they are financing is no longer valuable and will quite often request (or demand) that the survivor give them the insurance money to pay off the mortgage. If the survivor gives his insurance money to the mortgage company, he will not have money to rebuild. That could leave him with no place to live and no equity with which to start over. This affected so many people in the wildfires of Bastrop, TX in 2011 that the Texas Department of Emergency Management addressed the issue in the "Lessons Learned" section of their "Texas Long Term Recovery Guide."[3]

A better plan is to work with the mortgage company to set up an escrow account with the insurance money. The homeowner continues to make the same regular payments on the mortgage while drawing from the escrow account to rebuild or repair the house. The mortgage company does not lose their regular income, and they have the assurance that the insurance money is being used to protect their collateral. When the process is complete, the insurance money paid for the new construction, the homeowner still has their home, and the mortgage company continued to receive their payments. This is what worked for us. It was not easy.

---

3.   Published by Texas Department of Public Safety, Texas Division of Emergency Management, April 2015.

I was on the phone for many hours and wrote many letters to the mortgage company to make it work, but it was worth it.

A Tale of Two Very Different Cities

In the same week as West's explosion, a bomb was detonated at the Boston Marathon. No discussion about financial lessons learned during West's recovery would be complete without including the tale of these two very different cities.

Both cities experienced disastrous explosions in which lives were lost, people were injured, and property was damaged. The tragedies happened within days of each other, so the two cities shared headlines for a few weeks in April of 2013. That is where the similarities end. During our recovery some people unfairly compared the two tragedies and suggested that both cities could have used the same process to distribute donations and facilitate recovery. In fact, the two cities and the two experiences were so different that it was nonsensical to suggest that they should have, or could have, responded to their challenges in the same ways.

Boston is a large city with many resources, while West is a small town with limited resources. Boston is an historic, world-famous metropolitan community in the northeast; West is a relatively unknown rural community in central Texas. The explosion in Boston was caused by a bomb that was intentionally detonated, but the one in West was caused by a fire at a fertilizer storage facility. The Boston bombing was an act of terrorism, so it was correctly viewed as an attack on the whole nation. The fertilizer plant explosion in West was a terrible accident and seen as a local disaster. While the number of injuries was comparable (approximately 260 in each event), Boston had three fatalities, and West had 15. The differences in property damage were remarkable. In West, over 160 homes were destroyed, about 50 homes had major damage, and another 50 reported minor damage. West Independent School District lost three out of four school campuses. The City of West had approximately $13 million in damage to the city infrastructure and our communications tower. We also lost our EMS building, hospital authority, nursing home (which was the second largest employer in town), a handful of small businesses, and two historic meeting halls. By comparison, the property damage in Boston was negligible.

Due to the nature of the tragedy in Boston, the media coverage of it, and the general sense that it was an attack on the nation, donations quickly flowed into Boston. West, however, was not very well known, and its disaster was not a national attack. The explosion in West happened two days after the Boston bombing and two days before the dramatic manhunt for the bombers, so the nation's attention was understandably on Boston when the tragedy in West occurred. As a result of these factors, West received about 17 times less than Boston in donations. Boston received approximately $69.8 million for victims' relief, while West received about $3.6 million. (These figures represent money donated to the primary funds that were established for victims and their families and do not include FEMA, state funding, or donations made to churches, charities, or other organizations.) The financial losses in Boston were far less than those in West, but the donations received were far greater for Boston. That is understandable and reasonable, so I am not complaining about what we received. Instead, my goal is to demonstrate the vast differences in our recoveries. While no amount of money is ever enough to fully cover all the needs after a disaster, Boston received abundant resources, while West received much less than we needed. Therefore, we had to find ways to stretch our funds and make sure people used their insurance, FEMA, and other resources before drawing from our recovery funds.

In Boston, the mayor and the governor coordinated efforts to establish One Fund Boston, which had the power and personnel to expedite creating a new charity and obtaining the 501(c)(3) status from the IRS. They were then able to put all the victims into four or five broad categories. If a family fit the criteria of the first category, they received a specific amount of money. If someone fit the criteria for the second category, they received the specified amount for that category, etc. By contrast, our losses were much more varied. Since we had so many kinds of losses that varied so greatly in monetary value, it would not have been fair or efficient for us to use broad categories for distribution.

One of the most important differences in our town's experiences was the role of the city government. In Boston, the city officials were instrumental in establishing the charity and in conducting the work throughout the distribution process. In West, the only city employee who had the ability to coordinate efforts like that would have been our City Manager, Joey Pustejovsky. Joey was not only our City Manager, but he was also one of our volunteer firefighters, and he gave his life protecting our city when the explosion happened. When we lost Joey, we also lost our key city administrator. In small towns like ours, the mayor and city council serve as volunteers. Our mayor Tommy Muska, mayor pro tempore Steve Vanek, and the aldermen who make up our city council did an amazing job leading us through our recovery, but we simply did not have the personnel or infrastructure to do what Boston could do.

There is a significant difference between how municipalities and non-profits can distribute money. Not long after I joined the board of the West, TX Foundation, I got frustrated because I wanted to start handing out money to anyone who needed it, but a non-profit is not allowed to function that way. The IRS requires disaster recovery charitable organizations to "make a specific assessment that a recipient of aid is financially or otherwise in need."[4] We had to use case workers to guide our survivors through a process of demonstrating their needs after receiving insurance and FEMA assistance. That process takes time for several reasons, not the least of which is each household has to hear from FEMA before their unmet needs can be assessed by case workers.

Recognizing the differences between the two cities is more than trivial. Some in the media made ridiculous comparisons during the two recoveries because the disasters occurred in the same week. Most of those who reported on the contrasting recoveries failed to explain the reasons why the two recoveries could not have happened in the same ways. That part of the story needed to be told.

4.   Internal Revenue Service Publication 3833, (Rev. 7-2009), Catalog Number 32168V, p. 11.

CHAPTER 9
INTERACTING WITH MEDIA

Share your story and give God the glory.

If you have to help your community get through disaster recovery, you will most likely be approached by members of the media. Each leader must decide whether she wants to talk to the media or not. Doing interviews or responding to media requests is not something most of us have much experience doing, so you may not be comfortable with it. You are under no obligation to speak to the media, but there are some benefits to doing so if you are comfortable with it. The night of our explosion, I saw our little town on the national news. That let me know we had captured the media's attention, and they would soon be arriving. I decided early on that I would talk with the media and be as helpful to them as I could. I made that decision for three reasons. One was spiritual, another was practical, and the third was tactical.

First, it was clear that our tragedy was going to give us a voice. People all over the nation and beyond were watching and listening to what was happening in our little town. I felt called to use that platform to direct people's attention to God. I wanted to use every opportunity I was given to describe how God was working and how He was helping us in our time of need. I chose to cooperate with the media because I hoped to bring God glory. Psalm 71:15 became an important word of testimony for me: "My mouth will tell of your righteous acts, of your deeds of salvation all the day, for their number is past my knowledge." In a similar way, David spoke of the joy of celebrating God's goodness in Psalm 145:4: "One generation shall commend your works to another, and shall declare your mighty acts." I am also reminded of Jairus' daughter. The story of Jesus raising her from the dead appears in all three synoptic gospels. Jesus sent the crowd out of the room so that only the parents and the disciples were there. After restoring her to life, Jesus told everyone in the room not to tell anyone what they had seen Him do.[1] Matthew's account then adds, "News of this spread through all that region" (9:26 NIV). Apparently, someone in that room could not keep a secret. One of the parents, or perhaps one of the disciples, was so amazed and blessed by what Jesus had done, they could not help themselves and had to tell somebody. That is how I felt as I looked around me and watched God caring for our community, providing for our needs, bringing us together, and helping us heal. I wanted to spend the rest of my life telling stories of His goodness. I did a few interviews, responded to many emails, and had a few opportunities to speak to churches and civic groups. I thought the rest of my life would be spent telling our story and giving God glory. What I did not anticipate, however,

---

1. Jesus did this on numerous occasions following miracles. He did not want everyone to know He was Messiah until the right moment, and that moment had not yet come.

was that people got tired of hearing about it long before I got tired of talking about it.

The second reason I chose to cooperate with the media as much as I could was that I saw it as an opportunity to remind potential donors and volunteers that we still needed help. I wanted to show people that we were using their donations and making good progress, but we were still in need. I knew the news cycle turns quickly, and the media would move on to other stories soon, but by cooperating with the reporters, I could keep their attention on West a little longer, which would lead to more donations coming in.

Third, reporters are always going to report something. Whether they are on TV, radio, the internet, or in print, they all have to submit their stories to bosses who are expecting them to have something to report. Since I knew they were going to say *something*, I wanted to give them something to say. If I chose not to answer questions or tell them our story, I would have no influence on the message they were broadcasting. I wanted the reports coming out of West to be positive, hopeful, and accurate. Therefore, it was important to me to work with the media so I could do all I could to bring God glory, to remind people to keep helping us, and to help ensure that reporting from West was factual.

As I gave interviews, answered questions, responded to phone calls and emails, etc., I learned some helpful lessons about working with the media.

Ride the Wave

The term "news cycle" refers to the period of time between the publication or broadcast of a news story and when that story is replaced by another. I have noticed that prolonged stories, like disaster recovery, have their own ebb and flow. Instead of a news cycle, big stories that are worthy of follow-up reports have a news wave. Stories that begin as bad news will transform into stories about good news and then return to bad news. This is driven by the nature of news media. In order for a reporter to make their name in the business, they must have stories that make them stand out from the other reporters. So, if things are going well, they report on bad news items. Once everyone gets on that bandwagon, the time comes for the reporter to change things up and report on good news again. Success in reporting depends on being different than everyone else in the field, so we ride the wave. Good news leads to bad and bad to good.

Stories like disasters begin with bad news. The media covers the losses, the damage, the casualties, and the heartache. Soon after that, as the community begins that first climb in the emotional response chart (described in Chapter 6), the stories become good news. Reports of cooperation, volunteerism, and heroism catch people's attention. Then, in order to keep interest going, reporters change it up and find negative things to report about. If you are a leader in recovery, you just have to ride that wave. Utilize every opportunity afforded you while the wave is running high. When it dips down and the news becomes difficult to hear, hang on. It will turn up again.

Avoid the Trap

When you participate in an interview, just relax and be yourself. It is the reporter's job to help you think of what to say. Her questions should feed you what you need to tell the story or stress your points. After each question, pause for a couple of seconds to breathe and think, then talk to the reporter like you would talk to another person if there were no camera there. Look at the reporter, not the camera.

While you do want to stay relaxed and have a normal conversation, there is one question that I recommend you answer very carefully or not at all. Occasionally, a reporter will ask something like, "As you look back at how you have handled things so far, is there anything you would do differently?" While it might be an innocent question, there are many other possible scenarios of which you need to be aware. That question could be planned as a "gotcha" question. A "gotcha" question seems innocuous enough, but it is intended to get you to say something that can be used against you later. By talking about what you could have done differently, you are admitting to some level of fault. That may be exactly what you need to do, but if you do not intend it to be an admission of failure or mistakes, tread lightly. The question could even be used as a trap to get you to say something that could become a soundbite and used as evidence in a lawsuit.

If you are asked a question like this, consider either using an answer that does not put you in a vulnerable position or just saying you don't have an answer to that question. I was once asked that question on camera, and the hairs on my neck stood up. I became keenly aware that the interview might not be what it seemed to be. Something about it did not feel genuine, so I replied that I felt good about the decisions and actions we had made so far, given the information and resources we had at the time. The interview ended quickly after that, which confirmed for me that the person asking questions was most likely hoping to get a soundbite instead of sincerely trying to learn something from our experience.

Expect the Challenges

Over the past decade, I have talked with many reporters. I can say without hesitation that almost all of them were friendly, thoughtful, and professional. I have great appreciation for the members of the news media. They serve a valuable and essential role in our society, and most of them with whom I have worked fulfill that role with integrity. There are, however, some challenges that are inherent in modern media. Pastors and ministry leaders endeavoring to lead their communities through difficult times cannot do much to avoid these challenges, but it is important to be ready for them.

One such challenge is that a reporter can quote anyone as saying anything, and that quote is often perceived by the public to be truth. When including a quote, a hard-working, ethical reporter will do the work necessary to obtain clarification from someone on the other side of the issue or will include quotes from both sides. Some reporters do not go to that much trouble. For example, if the point of their story is to show that a conflict has arisen in a community, all they need to do is interview or quote someone who is upset and that becomes the story. The problem occurs when the viewing public assumes that one-sided, skewed perspective represents the truth. A report can be factual without being truthful. If the reporter claims, "Mrs. Peabody told us that the circus elephants were pink and could dance on their hind legs," that may be a factual report of what Mrs. Peabody said. That does not mean, however, that the elephants are indeed pink or that they can dance on their hind legs. The reporter did not claim the elephants could dance; he only claimed that Mrs. Peabody made her statement. Quoting someone is safe for the reporter because the reporter is being accurate, but it can also be misleading if it does not adequately present the whole truth.

Another challenge for which leaders should prepare is that many reporters basically write their stories before they even show up. The interview, then, is just intended to gather some soundbites that support the story they want to tell. We had one reporter from *The Washington Post* who was aware of that common practice and intentionally avoided it. He came to town about a year after the explosion and stayed for a few days. He said he wanted to meet the people, experience the culture, and discover what stories were here that should be told. When his report was published, it was one of the best works done on our recovery.

On the other extreme, we had a reporter who came to a press conference on the day that we announced we had finally received the long-term recovery funds and were beginning to distribute them. It was supposed to be a good news day, but the reporter came with another agenda. After the press conference, she ambushed me on camera and asked if there was a man who was being evicted from the temporary housing he was using during recovery. I was about to explain that I did not know what she was talking about but would be glad to find out what I could and get back to her about it. Before I could speak, a lady jumped in front of the camera and started screaming about how her friend had been mistreated and was being kicked out of the hotel where he was staying. That let me know that the whole thing was planned ahead of time. The lady from West had clearly contacted the reporter beforehand, and the reporter had planned her story based on the information the lady had given her. I saw they were creating the story they wanted to tell and had not really intended to ask me for helpful information, so I moved out of the way and let them do their thing.

The reporter represented a station that broadcasts in Spanish, and over the next few days, I got several calls from people asking why we were not taking care of the Hispanic people in our community. I assured them that was not the case. The accusations of racism based on that report hurt me deeply. I asked a few questions of our case workers and easily discovered that we were not involved in the situation at all. The man had asked a national charitable organization for financial assistance to stay at the local hotel. That group approved his request and told him how much they could give him. They clarified the date that his money would run out and told him he would need to make plans for his next step before that date arrived. When that time came, their agreement was concluded, and he had to leave the hotel. The lady who was concerned about her friend never came to us to ask for help on his behalf, and the news reporter did not even try to find out if we had any responsibility in his short-term plan. This unfortunate, extreme example demonstrates what can happen when reporters write their stories before they conduct interviews or do research.

Stick the Landing

In gymnastics, an athlete can have a near-perfect routine, but everyone sits on the edge of their seat and holds their breath until the very last moment of the routine. The success or failure of the performance seems to rely on that landing. If the routine went well and the athlete "sticks the landing," the crowd erupts with applause.

The landing of an interview will not make or break your performance, but it is important. You can count on the final question being pretty much the same in almost every interview. If you are prepared for it, you can stick that landing. Almost every interview I ever did ended with the reporter asking some version of, "Is there anything else you want to say that I did not ask you about?" It is an open-ended, free opportunity to make sure you and the reporter covered everything of importance.

I usually declined and told the reporter they had done such a good job that I was sure they had covered everything. Sometimes, however, I would use that opportunity to remind the reporter that God had been good to us and was helping us through the recovery. Since you know that will most likely be the final question in an interview, you might want to think about it and plan ahead. Have a key idea or main message in mind. If you do not get to present that key idea adequately during the interview, bring it up in your answer to the final question.

I wish I had utilized that final question more effectively because there is an issue in our story that no one has ever asked me about, but I think needs to be addressed. There is a disconnect between urban and rural living that has caused some confusion, and I did not realize that was happening until I no longer had a platform on which to address it. We always called the facility that blew up the "fertilizer plant." Actually, it was not a plant but a storage facility. When people in big cities hear "plant," they picture manufacturing facilities with big smokestacks and machinery working around the clock with multiple shifts of employees coming and going. Our fertilizer facility was a little "mom and pop" company that probably had a dozen employees. Nothing was manufactured there. The materials and chemicals

111

were shipped in and stored. Local farmers would then come by and order fertilizer that was made with 70% of this and 20% of that and 10% of something else. Those ingredients were mixed, and the fertilizer was ready to go. When people in big cities or urban areas heard about our "fertilizer plant," they could not understand how the city grew up so close to it. They imagined the kinds of manufacturing plants they see in industrial areas outside their big cities. In rural Texas, having a fertilizer storage facility close to small towns is not uncommon, particularly if those towns are still primarily agricultural communities like West.[2]

That concluding question in an interview would have been a good opportunity for me to clear up some of the misunderstanding between big city life and rural life. I wish I had thought of it when I had the chance.

---

2.   Fortunately, other rural communities like ours have learned some valuable lessons from our experience and have made some important adjustments to storage procedures and inspection policies.

CHAPTER 10
TOMORROW IS
ON THE WAY

"Deliverance is to the Bible what jazz music is to Mardi Gras...
bold, brassy, and everywhere." Max Lucado [1]

Thanks to the dedication, sacrifice, and hard work of the West ISD administration, faculty, staff, and school board, West students only missed two days of school after the explosion. Although we lost our high school, middle school, and intermediate school all at once that Wednesday night, our kids were back in school Monday morning. Our intermediate students were crowded into the elementary school. Connally ISD allowed our middle school and high school students to use one of their buildings. When our students arrived at the Connally building, they were greeted by Connally Cadets welcoming them to a building that had been repainted West red instead of Connally blue.

That Monday morning, I drove by the elementary school on my way to work. I will always remember what I saw there.

---

1.   Max Lucado, *You'll Get Through This: Hope and Help for Your Turbulent Times*, (Nashville: Thomas Nelson, 2013), 9.

Children were running and playing and laughing. That laughter spoke volumes to me. All weekend we had dealt with pain, suffering, fear, and loss, but suddenly, there was some hope. Those joyful children reminded me we did have a future. I remember thinking about how terrible the past few days had been, but what a relief it was to know that tomorrow was on the way.

The last half of Psalm 30:5 reminds us, "Weeping may tarry for the night, but joy comes with the morning." When you are in crisis, trying to survive, you just hope for one more breath. As the crisis subsides, you see the devastation left behind and feel the sorrow of loss and the pain of destruction. Your world has changed, and everything appears to be broken. When you find yourself in that lonely darkness, hold on. Remember, one of these days, very soon, you will notice a glimmer of light slowly peeking over the horizon. That dim light on the horizon will gradually become brighter, and eventually, a new day will dawn. As Max Lucado reminds us so brilliantly in the title of his excellent book, "you'll get through this."[2]

"Through" is a great word. We wish we did not have to be in the darkness of disaster and recovery, but the good news is we will not always be in it. We will get through it. In the most beloved Psalm, David declares, "The LORD is my shepherd" (Psalm 23:1), which later allows him to profess, "Even though I walk through the valley of the shadow of death, I will fear no evil, for you are with me..." (Psalm 23:4a). David knew that with the Shepherd as his guide, he would make it through the valley. He sang not of sitting in the valley or quitting in the darkness but of going through it.

2. Lucado, *You'll Get Through This*, 9.

When God's people were in exile and facing great difficulty, they most likely felt abandoned, but through the prophet Isaiah, God reassured them: "When you pass through the waters, I will be with you; and through the rivers, they shall not overwhelm you; when you walk through fire you shall not be burned, and the flame shall not consume you" (Isaiah 43:2).[3] I like the word "through," but I do not like the word "when." I wish the scriptures talked about *if* you go through the valley or *if* you go through floods and fires. But that is not what it says. Throughout scripture, we learn that we will face difficulties at some point. We need not wonder *if* they will happen; we need to be ready *when* they happen. Jesus even taught His disciples, "In the world you have tribulation, but take courage; I have overcome the world" (John 16:33b NASB). We live in a messed up, mixed up world where tragedies happen, good people suffer, and disasters disrupt our lives. The good news is we can get through those times. A new day will come, and there will be joy again. "Joy comes with the morning" (Psalm 30:5). You may not be able to see the sunrise yet, but it is on the way. The sun will rise, the darkness will fade, and a new day will dawn. While you wait, trust in the Lord; watch and listen for His presence.

I confess that I am not much of a music person. I know what I like to hear, but I cannot tell you why I like it. All my siblings are musicians, but I think the music gene got dropped by the time my parents got to me. Music is not just something that sounds good or bad to my family. It makes them feel things, and it is a means of communication for them. I usually miss out on that level of experience when I hear a song. When I was going through the darkest days of recovery, however, God spoke to me through music.

---

3. See the sermon starter "Through Floods and Fires" in the appendix.

The first time happened when I was driving to my temporary home after one of my many long, hard days. I was physically exhausted, emotionally drained, and spiritually weak. Then I heard a new song come on the radio, and I had to pull over on the shoulder of FM 1858 and weep. "Worn"[4] had been released about nine months earlier, but this was the first time I heard it. Tenth Avenue North captured my experience and put into words what I could not express on my own. The song includes a confession of feeling utterly worn out and begging that God will send the assurance of redemption. In small increments, God began to answer that prayer, and I started seeing His mighty hand at work in me and around me. I was healing and wanted to honor God and worship Him again, but I knew I was not whole and could not give God what He deserved. That is when I heard "Broken Hallelujah" by The Afters.[5] It was released three days after our explosion. Again, the words enabled me to express what I was experiencing but had no language to communicate. All I had to offer God at that time was my brokenness, but I would faithfully give Him all I had left. As I gained strength and realized I was growing, I discovered Mandisa's newly released victory anthem "Overcomer."[6] Those three songs were all released just before I needed to hear them. While I do not claim that the release of those songs was timed for me personally, I am convinced that God brought my attention to them at the very moment I needed them. In the same

---

4. Tenth Avenue North, "Worn," by Jason Ingram, Jeff Owen, and Mike Donehey, ©2012 Formerly Music, Open Hands Music, Prepare For The Zombie Apocalypse, So Essential Tunes, Spirit Nashville Three.

5. The Afters, "Broken Hallelujah," by Dan Ostebo, Jordan Mohilowski, Josh Havens, and Matt Fuqua, ©2013 Screaming Mimes Music, Smells Like Music, Songs For Miles, Demo Love, Miracle In My Hand Music.

6. Mandisa, "Overcomer," by Ben Glover, Chris Stevens, and David Garcia, ©2013 Universal Music— Brentwood Benson Publishing, 9T One Songs, Ariose Music, Meaux Mercy, Moody Producer Music, D Soul Music.

way, the day I watched my damaged home being demolished, I got back in the car and turned on the radio just in time to hear Building 429 singing "Where I Belong."[7] That powerful chorus kept reminding me that this temporary dwelling was not where I ultimately belong, but as Paul taught us, I have a "house not made with hands, eternal in the heavens" (2 Corinthians 5:1b).

God may not choose to use music to guide you through your journey but remember that He is at work even when you cannot see it. He is working to bring order to the chaos and beauty from the ashes (Isaiah 61:3). "And we know that for those who love God all things work together for good, for those who are called according to his purpose" (Romans 8:28). You will once again be able to lift your face to the heavens. Your song will return. Your load will get lighter. The darkness will fade, and a new day will dawn. Tomorrow is on the way.

---

7.   Building 429, "Where I Belong," by Jason Ingram and Jason Roy, ©2010 Spirit Nashville Three, Be Essential Songs, Havery Publishing, So Essential Tunes, Spirit Nashville Three.

APPENDIX: SERMON STARTERS

"Preach the word; be ready in season and out of season..."
2 Timothy 4:2a

Amid the chaos, stress, and long hours of disaster recovery, it can be difficult for a preacher to plan and prepare sermons, but the people in your church will be more receptive than ever to hearing a word from the Lord. The following sermon starters are intended to give pastors and teachers a few ideas to help in preaching through recovery. They are only sketches because the sermons will be yours. I hope they can provide a few starting points that will help you preach or teach through some of the most difficult times your church family will endure.

"Tears in a Bottle"
Psalm 56:8 (NASB95)

1. **"You have taken account of my wanderings."** After a disaster, it feels like we are just wandering around in a confused fog or haze. God is walking through this experience with us.

2. **"Put my tears in Your bottle."** Tear ducts are our pressure relief valves. God cares enough to pay attention to every tear that drops from our eyes.

3. **"Are they not in Your book?"** Remember, you only keep a record of things that are important. Our wanderings and our tears must be important to our Father if He keeps track of them. That's how much He cares.

   Think about those tears: "Jesus wept" (John 11:35). If it's OK for Him, it's OK for me. One of these days, God is going to set down my bottle and reach down with His hand of compassion and wipe away my last tear (Revelation 21:4).

"Arise and Build"
Nehemiah 1:1–4

Like Nehemiah, let's start dreaming about how we might rebuild. Vision provides the push to get through the problems, the energy for the effort, the passion for the purpose.

Today, let us not see the destruction of yesterday but the glory of tomorrow.

1. Ask questions about the way things are (v.2).

2. Admit the seriousness of the problems (v.3).

3. Allow yourself to be affected by the problems (v.4).

4. Acknowledge your need for God's help (v.4b).

"Beauty for Ashes"
Isaiah 61:1–4

1. The Glorious Proclamation (vs. 1–2)

- We are going to be OK! This is probably the most difficult thing we will ever face, but God is big enough to get us through it.

2. The Glorious Provision (v.3)

- He can turn endings into beginnings, mourning into joy, beauty into ashes.

- Why does He do it? To display His splendor.

3. The Glorious Promise (v.4)

- We will rebuild and renew our city.

- We will not only survive, but we will thrive again!

- We will rebuild by His grace and for His glory.

4. The Glorious Fulfillment (Luke 4:16–21)

- Can He really take ashes and bring beauty?

    Ask the woman at the well, blind Bartimeus, the lonely leper, the lame man, Lazarus, the centurion, Peter, Paul & Silas, and many others. For that matter, just ask me! "I once was lost but now I'm found."[1] I was broken, but now I'm whole. I was confused, but now I know the Truth. I was discouraged, but now I have hope. I was hurting, but now I have peace.

    Beauty for ashes—He can take a messy, mixed-up life and turn it into something beautiful, meaningful, and purposeful.

---

1.   John Newton, "Amazing Grace," 1779.

"I'm Not Homeless, I'm Just Not Home Yet"
2 Corinthians 4:16–5:7

1. A New Power (v.16)

- We will put our whole heart into our recovery and will not give up.

- God is renewing our strength every day.

- Every day I wake up is a gift—a gift I used to take for granted.

- Isaiah 40:29

2. A New Perspective (vs.17–18)

- Paul went through terrible times but saw his suffering as light compared to the weight of glory.

- The reason this is the worst thing we could imagine is that we've never seen anything worse. Life is relative.

- When we compare it to glory, this is a light, momentary affliction.

- Romans 8:18

3. A New Body (vs.5:1–4)

- Paul was a tentmaker. He refers to the tabernacle, which was a big tent—it was a mobile temple.

- The "glorified" body will have no decay or weakness.

- Philippians 3:20–21

4. A New Home (vs.6–7)

- I may not have a house, but I have a home!

- John 14:2

  I have a home prepared for me by the Great Creator Himself, and it's a home not made with hands, so it can't be blown up or torn down. It is eternal.

"Through Floods and Flames"
Isaiah 43:1–3a

1. Remember Who the Lord Is (v.1a)

- "Creator," "He who formed you"—He made you, He put you together. He knows your needs better than you do, and He knows how to meet those needs.

2. Remember Who You Are (v.1b)

- He told us not to fear the bad times, and He gave us three reasons not to fear.

  a. You are redeemed (He delivered you)

  b. You are called by name (He knows you personally)

  c. You are His (because He claims you)

3. Remember the Flames and Floods Will Come (v.2a)

- "when"—He assumes it's going to happen

  We live in a fallen, messed up world that is full of storms, dark valleys, floods, and flames.

  David understood that. Psalm 23:4 (KJV) says, "Yea though I walk through the valley…" I wish he had said, "*If* I go through the valley," but he said, "*when.*"

  John 16:33b (NASB): "In the world you have tribulation, but take courage; I have overcome the world."

4. Remember He is with You (v.3)

- The power of the presence of God is greater than any power in this fallen universe.

  Psalm 46:1: "God is our refuge and strength, a very present help in trouble."

Joshua 1:9: "Have I not commanded you? Be strong and courageous. Do not be frightened, and do not be dismayed, for the Lord your God is with you wherever you go."

5. Remember He Will Get You Through (v.3)

- "Through"—now that's a great word!

  Again, David said, "I walk *through* the valley..." (Psalm 23:4)

  You will face the fires and the floods, but you're not going to be in the flames or the water forever. By the power of His presence and the strength of His almighty hand, you will get through.

  Psalm 30:5b (NASB): "Weeping may last for the night, But a shout of joy comes in the morning."

- Conclusion

  Psalm 66:12b: "...we went through fire and through water; yet you have brought us out to a place of abundance."

"Worshiping When Times are Tough"
Habakkuk 3:16–18

1. Worship is a choice

2. Worship is about focus

3. Worship is about Him

"Lost and Found"
Luke 15

Celebrate some of the things that have been found in the rubble—sentimental things that mean so much to people. Then turn to Luke 15 where there are three more stories about things that were "Lost and Found." To understand the chapter, you need to look at all three stories and look at why Jesus told them (see 15:1–2). Jesus told the stories to help the people understand how God sees the lost and the found.

- Two Lessons About Being Lost

1. Jesus cares about those who are lost.

2. When you're lost, you are not where you belong (sheep not in pen, coin not in purse, son not home).

- Two Lessons About Being Found

1. Salvation includes God's part and man's part.

   God takes the initiative, and man repents. See John 6:37

   The shepherd looked for the sheep, the woman looked for the coin, the father looked for the son. The son eventually had to get out of the pig pen and go home.

2. God loves and forgives (like prodigal's father). See Psalm 103:10–13

Giving Thanks for the Blessings

Instead of preaching a sermon, just spend some time letting the people express gratitude to God for the blessings they have experienced during recovery. (Don't use this one too early. Let the people get through the short-term relief stage and be well into the long-term recovery phase.)

Winning Life's Battles
2 Chronicles 20

1. The Response of Victory (vs.3–4)
We can lose the battle before it begins if we respond to the enemy incorrectly. Jehoshaphat responded well.

2. The Recognitions of Victory (vs.5–6, 12–17)

  a. Who God Really Is (vs.5–6)

  b. We Must Depend on God (v.12)

  c. Our Battles Belong to the Lord (vs.15–17)

3. The Reasons for Victory (vs.18–23)

  a. Worship (v.18)

  b. Faith (v.20)

  c. Praise (vs.21–23)

4. The Reality of Victory (vs.24–25)

5. The Results of Victory (vs.26–30)

  a. God Receives Glory (vs.26–29)

  b. We Experience Peace (v.30)

Facing Your Fears
Psalm 56:3

We've been through a scary experience. Fear is normal, natural, and even healthy. Fear is a good thing when it protects us but not when it is disabling.

God is still at work, and He has greater things in store for our community.

The most frequently repeated command in scripture is "Fear not."

1. **Dare to Change** (Paul on the Road to Damascus, Acts 9)

2. **Dare to Believe** (Paul and Silas in prison, Acts 16)

3. **Dare to Trust** (Paul and the sailors in the shipwreck, Acts 27)

  The message to our community is Paul's message to the sailors in Acts 27:24–25: We are going to be OK. Trust in Him!

New Beginnings
Ecclesiastes 3:3b

Celebrate the exciting time of new beginnings as the community rebuilds.

As we enter into the season of new beginnings, don't rush through it. Appreciate it.

Revelation 21:1–5

- God is all about new beginnings.

- The reason we have hope is because God makes all things new.

  (Take a quick survey of scriptures that show how many ways God makes things new.)

- We are seeing God make things new all around us. Have you let Him make you new?

SCAN HERE to learn more about
Invite Ministries—created to invite people to a deeper
faith and living relationship with Jesus Christ